REAL ESTATE
INVE$TMENT

IN THE PURSUIT OF BUILDING INCOME-PRODUCING ASSETS TO GROW YOUR WEALTH

INCOME

SAVINGS

ASSETS

WEALTH

NASSER SALEM ABOUZAKHAR

Cover image by: Yesna99 – 99designs.com
Book design by: SWATT Books Ltd – swatt-books.co.uk

Printed in the United Kingdom
First Printing, 2021

ISBN: 978-1-9989984-0-1 (Paperback)
ISBN: 978-1-9989984-1-8 (eBook)

Nasser Abouzakhar
Manchester, M32 8HU

Dedication

To Yema d Baba who passed away in 2020 and 2017.

To my wife Fathia and my adult sons Adrar, Axcel, and Efaow and daughter Natir the youngest; without their support, this book would not have been written.

Acknowledgements

Many people helped me make this book possible, and I offer my thanks to all of them. I would like to thank my family for the pleasurable life I have and for their tireless support and love throughout my life. Fathia my wife, thanks for her patience, encouragement, and understanding while I was working on this book. She was able to make challenging times enjoyable. Fathia and my adult sons have played a significant role in making this adventure happen and completing this project. Their constructive comments and feedback on the selected topics and elaborated ideas are highly appreciated. They are very supportive business partners.

Thanks to Karen Williams my mentor for her magnificent advice and encouragement. Karen has been an outstanding resource and her help has been invaluable. This book would not have been completed without the support of Sam Pearce my publisher and Louise Lubke Cuss the book editor who played a significant role in making sure that everything is in the right order, thanks for your help and guidance. I also would like to thank Aline Hoareau for her important comments and constructive criticism on reviewing the book and Nick Stanton for his invaluable review.

I also express my deepest gratitude to my beloved family members back home in Libya for their love and endless support.

Praise for Real Estate Investment

Former cyber security lecturer turned property investor, Nasser offers a unique perspective on what it takes to succeed in the property investment world. In his book, Nasser shares his extensive experience and macro-economic insights, providing aspiring investors with all the tools they need.

Aline Hoareau, property investor

A factual, real time step by step guide to property investment. With clear and concise instructions and tips that will benefit the first time or experienced investor.

Nick Stanton, property expert

Contents

Abbreviations

AFFO Adjusted Funds from Operations

BMV Below Market Value

BREEAM Building Research Establishment's Environmental Assessment Method

BTL Buy-to-Let

CBD Central Business District

CGT Capital Gains Tax

CPI Consumer Price Index

CRA Credit Reference Agency

DIP Decision in Principle

EPC Energy Performance Certificate

FCA Financial Conduct Authority

GDP Gross Domestic Product

GHG Greenhouse Gas

HMO Housing of Multiple Occupancy/Occupation

HMRC HM Revenue & Customs

LTV Loan-to-value

MITR Mortgage Interest Tax Relief

NAV Net Asset Value

NBFI Non-bank Financial Institutions

NRLA National Residential Landlord Association

ONS Office of National Statistics

OPM Other People's Money

PED Price Elasticity of Demand

PES Price Elasticity of Supply

PIN Property Investor Network

PRA Prudential Regulation Authority

REIT Real Estate Investment Trust

RHI Renewable Heat Incentive

ROI Return on Investment

SA Serviced Apartment

SDLT Stamp Duty Land Tax

SVR Standard Variable Rate

SWOT Strengths, Weakness, Opportunities & Threats

UKHPI UK House Price Index

Introduction

Every year UK financial institutions secure billions of pounds to fund remortgage projects and the purchase of houses by individuals. These huge funds give individuals the opportunity to invest in buy-to-let properties, develop refurbishment projects, raise funds, and build income-producing portfolios. Lenders often expect investors to reinvest any raised funds by buying more income-producing properties. This should help investors grow their property portfolios, improve their businesses, and produce bigger returns. This book aims to help readers learn how real estate investment works using an easy-to-understand approach. It covers the core principles of investing and financing a real estate business and introduces various topics related to property investment. The topics included in this book are relevant to individuals who would like to understand how to develop their own property investment, whether in their family home or a property portfolio. The book is also useful to university students taking real estate investment, finance, and property economics-related courses.

It covers the core principles of investing and financing a real estate business and introduces various topics related to property investment.

As a director for a real estate investment company, I have tried to make use of my professional experience to discuss various topics and real-life scenarios to help individuals who are planning to start their property investment journey, set up a real estate business, and build their own property portfolios. The book presents the main issues that investors need to be aware of when they buy income-producing properties. Various tools and techniques are introduced to help investors evaluate market conditions and economic trends to plan their future investments and make the right investment decisions. The book highlights the importance of property location, how investors can select their best deals, and how investing in different asset classes offers investors the opportunity of getting high returns. Therefore, the content provides useful information to help beginners succeed in addressing market and funding challenges and make better financial decisions.

The book covers the concepts of real estate economics such as property cycle, supply and demand, and how they influence property prices. It introduces the principles of property investment and the subjects of real estate finances, business philosophy, and market assessment, supported with useful examples. To help students understand the subject of sustainability in real estate investment, this book includes information accompanied by real-life scenarios and examples to help readers gain background knowledge about property investment and economics, estate agents, and risk management. It describes in detail the investment process used by property investors to build their portfolios. So the book should help beginners and students not only to become employable in the real estate industry but also how to become self-employed investors in the future if they want to. It should also provide useful information for those who are already in the property business, to gain more knowledge and use as a reference.

It introduces the principles of property investment and the subjects of real estate finances, business philosophy, and market assessment, supported with useful examples.

The real estate market depends on the economic situation in terms of property cycle and supply and demand which can influence property prices and investment, as well as market conditions. Economic factors such as unemployment, household income, interest rates, etc. as well as inflation do play a role in causing shifts in the supply and demand curves and thus shifts in the market. Inflation can reduce the returns on an investment (ROI); an inflation rate of 3% after an investment return of 2.8% will produce a negative return (2.8% − 3% = -0.2%). This sometimes makes the real estate rental market risky due to economic factors or unexpected events such as COVID-19 which could lead to irregularity in the property cycle. These challenges could have an impact on real estate investment and businesses in general. Therefore, investors have to use various tools and techniques to evaluate market conditions and economic trends to plan their future investments.

In my company, Anzar Property Group, understanding the principles of the property cycle, the relationship between supply and demand and property prices and market conditions can help us make the right investment decisions. Also, knowing how to assess and analyse the real estate market helps us plan our investment strategies. Having a clear market picture helps to identify challenges and available opportunities. A housing market assessment depends on the quality of the information gathered, and therefore investors have to gain the necessary research skills and observations using the relevant technologies and tools to their advantage. A modified version of Porter's Five Forces model of Business Competition Analysis is presented in this book to show how to support real estate investors to determine market challenges, analyse the level of competition, and develop a competitive strategy. The modified Porter's model is also useful in understanding how the assessment of the real estate market is carried out effectively.

As an investment company, we heavily rely on banks to fund our real estate investment projects, raise and invest capital into income-producing assets, and/or other asset classes. The subject of real estate finances and business philosophy, and how the UK government deals with the sector, will be presented in this book. In real estate investment, property location can determine whether the price is above or below average. Investors should be aware of the importance of investment location, for example, its proximity to a CBD (central business district), local amenities, and attractions. Investing in properties located in good areas can generate substantial rental income, and/or promising capital gains.

Investing in different types of classes offers investors the opportunity to get high returns, capital gains, and/or dividends from REIT (Real Estate Investment Trusts) stock market shares. Asset diversification provides investors with the opportunity to achieve better business resilience, use multiple strategies, improve their portfolios and earnings, and reduce risk. Real estate tends to contribute to carbon emissions which could have an impact on climate change. However, one way to reduce energy consumption and greenhouse emissions is to consider investing in sustainable buildings to minimise losses and bring financial and social benefits.

Investors need to be aware of how to select the best deals based on the property situation and the seller's circumstances. They can obtain such information and support from estate agents. This requires certain skills such as communication and negotiation to effectively deal with estate agents since they are the main providers of such crucial services to investors. However, investors need to be well prepared before initiating any negotiations. This

---

In my company, Anzar Property Group, understanding the principles of the property cycle, the relationship between supply and demand and property prices and market conditions can help us make the right investment decisions.

Asset diversification provides investors with the opportunity to achieve better business resilience, use multiple strategies, improve their portfolios and earnings, and reduce risk.

book provides a dedicated chapter about how investors can deal effectively with estate agents, arrange viewings, and negotiate prices.

Creative finance is an important aspect of the real estate investment business. It is an intelligent way of structuring investment deals to accumulate a good-sized property portfolio. In Anzar Property Group, we use creative finance to raise capital from third-party institutions such as banks to fund our investment projects. This makes creative finance an important aspect of our real estate business and enables us to leverage and use the least amount of our own capital. Some real-life examples showing how the use of creative financing for property deals has helped in expanding portfolios will be presented in this book.

Financial accounting is as important as creative finance since both processes provide the necessary support for investors to expand their portfolios. Financial accounting for the real estate business is a process of producing and reporting financial records and transactions resulting from business operations over a specified period. The importance of property accounting and producing accurate financial statements, profit and loss reports, and balance sheets will be explained in this book. To achieve this, it is helpful for real estate investors or businesses to use accounting software tools such as Xero for effective reporting, accurate projections, and tax planning. Real estate investment requires not only effective finance and accounting operations but also careful risk analysis and management. Investors have to understand the risk associated with their investment and to be aware of the importance of investing in different asset classes to reduce any potential losses and maximise the likelihood of positive outcomes.

Managing debt and its associated costs such as remortgage fees and increased interest should be seriously considered by investors to reduce risk. Banks carry out checks on investors' affordability, credit history and reports to assess the financial status of potential borrowers and reduce banks' risk as well. There is no riskless investment so investors have to gain the necessary skills to deal with worst-case scenarios, withstand market fluctuations, and manage and keep the risk of failure to a minimum. This book dedicates the last chapter to risk management and tolerance.

> Creative finance is an important aspect of the real estate investment business. It is an intelligent way of structuring investment deals to accumulate a good-sized property portfolio.

> Managing debt and its associated costs such as remortgage fees and increased interest should be seriously considered by investors to reduce risk.

Real Estate Economics

1

The real estate market depends on the economic situation in general and on supply and demand in particular. Because of various economic factors, property prices increase and decrease in a cyclical manner which includes four phases: expansion, hyper supply, recession, and recovery. All four phases will be discussed in this chapter. Various factors that influence property investments as well as the supply and demand for real estate are determined by different economic factors, which can affect the property price. These economic factors and market conditions will be presented in this chapter; they are useful for property investors to understand in order to make the right investment decisions. The role of elasticity in supply and demand will also be presented using a graphical model to monitor market prices.

Property Cycle

Many events in our world recur naturally and repetitively during different periods such as rain, winds, floods, etc. In a similar way, due to various economic factors such as GDP, interest rates, population change, employment rates, etc. property prices also go up and down in a cyclical manner. The property cycle has four phases, as shown in figure 1.1. The changes in supply and demand of properties play a role in influencing the property market, subsequently shaping the property cycle. The four phases of the real estate cycle are as follows:

The changes in supply and demand of properties play a role in influencing the property market, subsequently shaping the property cycle.

- **Expansion:** After the market recovery this phase contributes to the rise of property and rent prices and construction activities. Also, the unemployment rates and vacancy levels fall. It is a good time for active investors who can oversee market fluctuations to remortgage their properties that have benefited from capital gains, release equity for reinvestment, and add more assets to their portfolios.

- **Hyper supply:** Overbuilding projects due to higher demand during the expansion phase often leads to the hyper supply of properties. During this phase occupancy rates and rents begin to fall because of lower demand. Property oversupply could lead to a housing bubble which can cause financial crises and major problems in the housing market and economy. However, investors who were careful with their investments in terms of selection of property location, high yield producing properties, and long-term lease agreements may choose to continue with their investment. They may decide not to sell despite the downturn and high risk.

- **Recession:** During the recession phase, demand, property price, rental income, employment rates, and occupancy rates fall. It is a tenants' market, so investors might find themselves in a position to offer discounts to retain their tenants or attract potential tenants. It is a good time for active investors to look for opportunities and make use of their skills to find bargains and BMV (below market value) properties for sale. However, making use of such opportunities requires a lot of planning and preparation.

- **Recovery:** In this phase, the property market and employment rates start to improve. During the recovery phase, the economy starts to pick up but property supply does not happen due to oversupply during the previous two phases. However, limited construction activities might begin when there is a demand for properties at certain locations. It is not too late for investors who are willing to take a risk to find good deals such as distressed properties, or commercial to residential conversion projects, or adding value to damaged properties and selling them during the next phase. A distressed property is a type of property whose owner is unable to keep up with regular mortgage payments. It is common for a distressed property to be offered for sale by the lender.

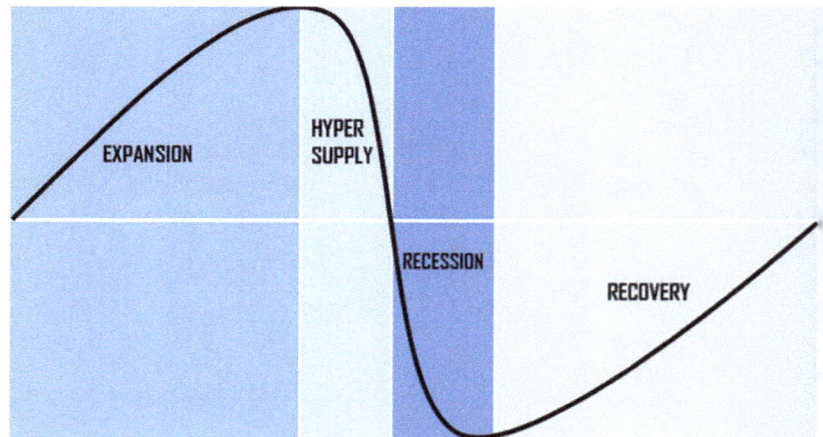

Figure 1.1 The four phases of the real estate cycle

At the peak and trough of the property cycle, both the supply and demand rates are equal. Although it is not easy to predict the length of each phase, active investors keep monitoring and examining the real estate cycle regularly. This is to figure out which of the cycles they are in and how to deal with the market changes at each cycle. Investors need to keep a close eye on the market's development to help them to:

Although it is not easy to predict the length of each phase, active investors keep monitoring and examining the real estate cycle regularly.

- Determine which phase of the real estate cycle they are in
- Identify business opportunities
- Plan their investment strategies and
- Make informed investment decisions

Sometimes unexpected events do happen without any prior knowledge which could cause irregularity to the repetitive cycle of real estate. The COVID-19 shock has brought the global economy to a near halt since early 2020. The lockdown measures by most countries, rise in unemployment rates, reduction in economic activities, and drop in GDP have had a knock-on effect on the real estate market and business growth.

Supply and Demand in the Property Market

Property prices and rents depend on the law of supply and demand in a free-market economy. The supply and demand mechanism in the property market is complicated. The demand for housing represents the number of residential properties buyers are willing to purchase at a certain price or that tenants are looking for to rent. The supply represents the construction and flow of residential properties available at a certain price. Prices and rent charges are determined by various economic factors that affect the property market. Factors that can greatly impact supply and demand might include the job market, interest rates, employment figures, demographic changes, etc.

Supply and demand for housing is a local market matter but influenced by various conditions as well as local, regional, and national regulations and policies. Like many countries, the UK's economy and government rely heavily on the property market, and hundreds of billions of overseas investments to generate income through tax and manage the country's deficit. Changes in property prices might not only affect property businesses' cash flow and investment, but also the country's economy as a whole including its credit rating and GDP. In his article in *The Independent* in 2017, Alexander Tziamalis stated that a 10 percent fall in the UK's property value would have a serious effect on the economy equivalent to more than 10 years of exported cars from the UK[1]. The main economic factors that affect the rise in price of properties in the UK are:

- Expensive land
- Limited housing development
- High development costs
- Limited social housing
- High demand

Decisions made by property investors, developers, local authorities, banks, and governments are also all responsible for price variations on the property market. The property market behaves in accordance with the relationship between supply and demand, which is influenced by price variations and the number of properties available in the market. Figure 1.2 shows how price influences supply and demand and vice versa. For example, when demand exceeds supply the price increases to a level known as an equilibrium state. The equilibrium state represents the price that matches the current demand to available supply. It represents a compromise between what buyers are willing to pay for properties and what sellers are willing to offer in terms of property specification and asking price.

> Changes in property prices might not only affect property businesses' cash flow and investment, but also the country's economy as a whole including its credit rating and GDP.

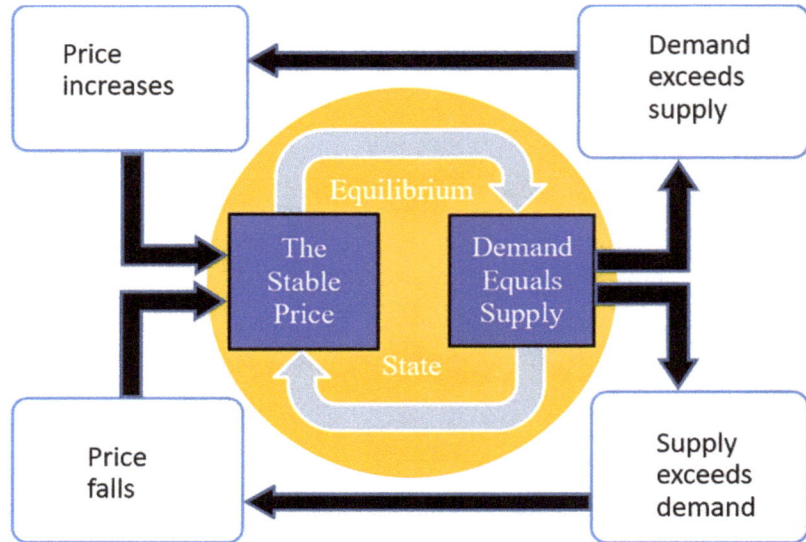

Figure 1.2 Demand, supply, and equilibrium

Relationship between Supply and Demand

In property economics, the supply and demand relationship represents the properties in the market that

- Sellers wish to sell or investors wish to invest in and offer to let at various prices and
- Buyers wish to buy or tenants wish to rent

This relationship is based on an economic theory used to model price determination in a market. Figure 1.3 shows the relationship between supply and demand. The horizontal x-axis represents the available stock and the vertical y-axis represents the property price or rent. Any change in the property price can be monitored along the demand curve and/or supply curve by holding constant all other non-price factors. However, any change in non-price factors would cause a shift in the demand curve and/or supply curve. The supply and demand curves intersect at the equilibrium or market-clearing price P1, Q1. Assuming the available property stock N1 would provide a price P1, the remaining stock i.e. above N1 represents the available stock.

Understanding the basic economic principles can help investors decide the best time to invest in properties. The property supply and demand relationship operates in the following three ways:

Understanding the basic economic principles can help investors decide the best time to invest in properties.

- The higher the demand, the lower the supply
- The higher the demand, the lower the number of properties that become available, and the higher the property price/rent. It is the sellers' or investors' market

- The lower the demand, the lower the property price and the higher the number of properties available i.e. the investors' market

Notice that investors are winning in both cases when there is high or low demand. Active investors can make use of the opportunity when property prices are high to remortgage and release equity, get funds to reinvest, and enlarge their portfolio. Also, they win when property prices are low by buying and investing in more properties at good prices, getting good bargains, even below market value (BMV).

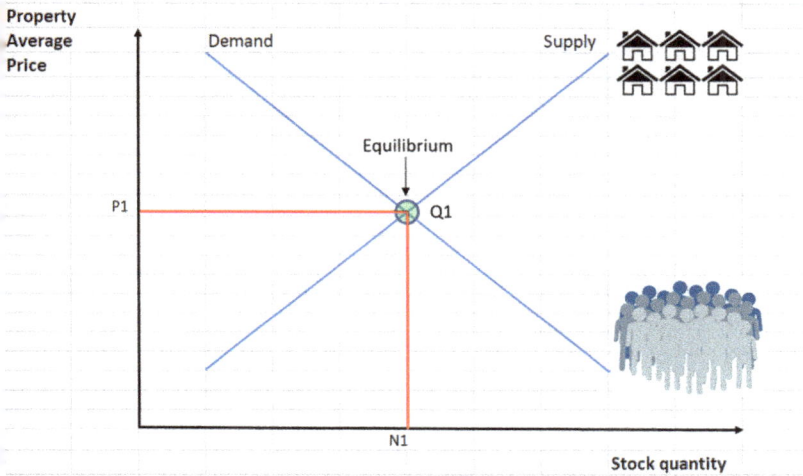

Figure 1.3 Supply and demand relationship

Elasticities of Supply and Demand

Elasticity is an indicator used to measure the variation of supply or demand following the variation of the price. Elastic demand means when people are very sensitive to price variations i.e. if the property price increases by a small amount, then the demand will decrease by a larger amount. This happens when property buyers have the option to buy less expensive houses and escape the highly-priced properties. Price Elasticity of Demand (PED) measures how sensitive buyer demand is to property price variation. According to MrBanks.co.uk[1], Price Elasticity of Supply (PES) measures the proportional change in property supplied due to a proportional change in property price.

It often requires a lot of time and effort to supply residential needs and to meet the demand by home buyers and tenants. Inelastic supply means that property investors have limited options for properties and cannot easily move to other areas to invest unless they decide to move their investment to other places or countries. The inelasticity of the supply curve and supply constraints occurs because of various factors:

It often requires a lot of time and effort to supply residential needs and to meet the demand by home buyers and tenants.

- Scarcity of developed land and costs
- Planning permission complexities and restrictiveness

- Property development regulations
- Construction delays
- Lending conditions
- Availability of skilled labour
- Competition
- Landscape
- Limited incentives and funding

Summary

Property prices increase and decrease in a cyclical manner due to various economic factors. This chapter covered the property cycle which includes four phases: expansion, hyper supply, recession, and recovery. The economic situation and its factors influence real estate market conditions, investment activities, and supply and demand. These economic factors and changes in market conditions are useful in enabling investors to make the right investment decisions. Therefore, the next chapter will introduce the relationship between supply and demand and their effects on real estate economies and prices. It will discuss the issue of property valuation and rental market dynamics due to the limited stock and the supply of real estate. Due to the importance of the issue of the shortage in housing stock and its implications for real estate supply and investment, the next chapter also covers the tools used by the UK government to deal with such challenges to resolve them.

Real Estate Market and Valuation

2

The relationship between supply and demand and their effects on real estate economics and prices will be covered in this chapter. I discuss how dynamic the rental market is due to limited stock and property supply. The issues of property valuation and pricing are also covered. In addition, property-related tax has implications on the real estate market, property prices, and supply and demand. The UK government faces various economic challenges because of the shortage in housing stock and limited supply. These challenges include increased demand and inflated prices for properties, green belt destruction, lack of skilled builders etc. Governments use taxation as a powerful tool to resolve such challenges. The final part of this chapter covers issues related to property and tax.

Property Price, Supply, and Demand

Property price is a determinant factor in the supply and demand for housing. Any price changes cause a movement along the demand curve, as shown in figure 2.1. There seems to be a direct relationship between house prices and demand. However, some non-price factors affect the level of demand for housing and how able and willing buyers are to pay the offered prices. They are:

Property price is a determinant factor in the supply and demand for housing.

- Household size and income
- Population
- Property area and location
- Regulations and legal requirements
- Demographics
- Interest rates
- Preferences
- Local amenities
- Infrastructure
- Public "goods" e.g. good schools

The non-price factors that influence the level of supply are:

- Cost of development
- Local council regulations
- Government laws
- Housing policies
- Labour cost
- Material cost

The property price is determined by the market i.e. comparable neigh-bouring properties and the ability to supply enough properties. It often requires a lot of time and effort to supply the market needs of real estate and to meet the demand. Property development projects take time to complete because of the development requirements and strict building regulations. Property prices tend to inflate where supply is constrained because of the inelasticity of the supply curve. Inelastic supply means that the supply of real estate is less sensitive to price changes. Also, limited options available to investors and developers drive property prices up. Figure 2.1 shows a more constrained supply. It shows that the supply curve is inelastic in comparison to the elastic demand curve. The supply curve is relatively steep (inelastic supply) i.e. the quantity supplied of properties is less sensitive to changes in price. Constraints of property supply affect property prices depending on how desirable the area is and the level of demand.

Constraints of property supply affect property prices depending on how desirable the area is and the level of demand.

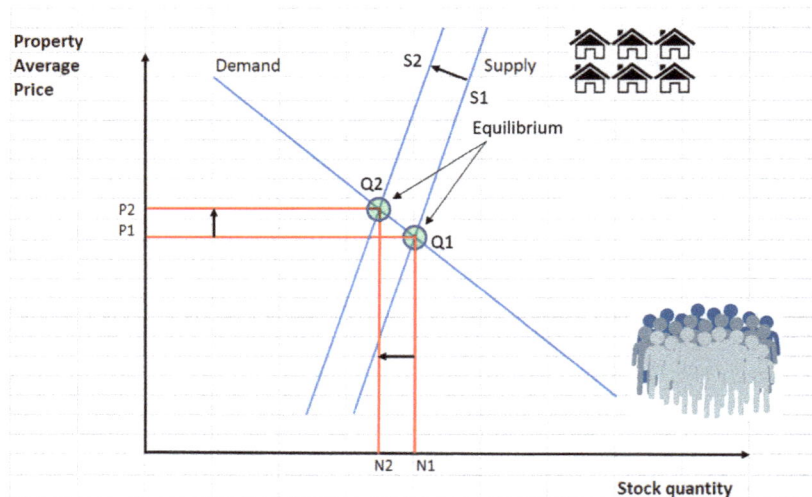

Figure 2.1 Supply reduced due to increased demand

It takes a long time for developers to find the right land for a project. It can take years to complete a new property development project. The planning process can affect project development as well. The increased cost of devel-opment has caused a shift in the supply curve from S1 to S2 as a movement along the demand curve, as shown in figure 2.1. The increased develop-ment cost has a knock-on effect on property supply and reduction in stock quantity. Therefore, a new equilibrium price P2 has been reached with some properties N2, and a new equilibrium point Q2 has been created. The increase in the property development cost has caused the equilibrium point to move from Q1 to Q2.

In the UK, housing policies benefit a variety of individuals in society such as owner-occupiers, first-time buyers, low-income households, elderly and disabled people, and tenants. For example, homeowners are exempt from SDLT (Stamp Duty Land Tax) when they sell their properties. Also, first-time buyers can benefit from the provision of additional support for the purchase of their first properties and to get on the property ladder. Housing policies play a significant role in providing social housing and the provision of housing for low-income households. Older and disabled people can benefit from housing policies in terms of getting the right support and to ensure that the housing on offer for them is suitable. Moreover, housing policies are often used to control the private rental sector and to give necessary support to tenants who live in rented properties.

The Rental Market and Property Supply

There is always a fixed number of properties available for new tenants or the investment market. Rental prices are determined by the supply and demand rate and often depend on comparable properties. However, the property market is dynamic due to various factors such as the movement of tenants, demolition of existing properties, and development of new properties. As a determinant factor, price is used to influence the demand and supply for the housing market. However, other factors such as population, unemployment, average household income, crime rate etc. are also important, and changes in these factors cause a shift in the supply and/or demand curves as well. According to economicsonline.co.uk[2], renting property is an alternative to ownership, and the demand for private housing is influenced by changes in rental prices.

During periods of higher demand, individuals will be paying higher rents due to limited supply or limited options. The market supply determines the existing available stock for tenants as well as investors. The increase in rent prices is an indication of a higher demand for housing. Similarly, if the number of properties available on the market is low, the demand would be high as people would find it difficult to find affordable houses. This could be due to limited investment, expensive building material or labour, lack of funding, or not enough land on which to build new properties. However, if the number of available properties is high, people would not be willing to pay high prices or rents due to the options available.

When the population increases, demand for housing becomes high as more people are looking for properties to buy or rent and are willing to pay market prices. This results in a shift in the demand curve from D1 to D2, as shown in figure 2.2. The increase in demand has created an excess supply of N1 and N2. It has also led to excess demand for more properties and rents increasing from P1 to P2. This encourages active investors to invest more in the BTL (buy-to-let) market and to increase their profits because there is too much demand for residential properties. Investors are encouraged to invest as rent prices increase which implies more profits. Investors would try to gradually increase the rents and/or property prices and shift the equilibrium occupancy from Q1 to Q2, where the supply matches the new level of demand. If rental prices are low, investors would be reluctant to invest in properties due to lower achievable yields, unless property prices become suitable for investment.

> The market supply determines the existing available stock for tenants as well as investors. The increase in rent prices is an indication of a higher demand for housing.

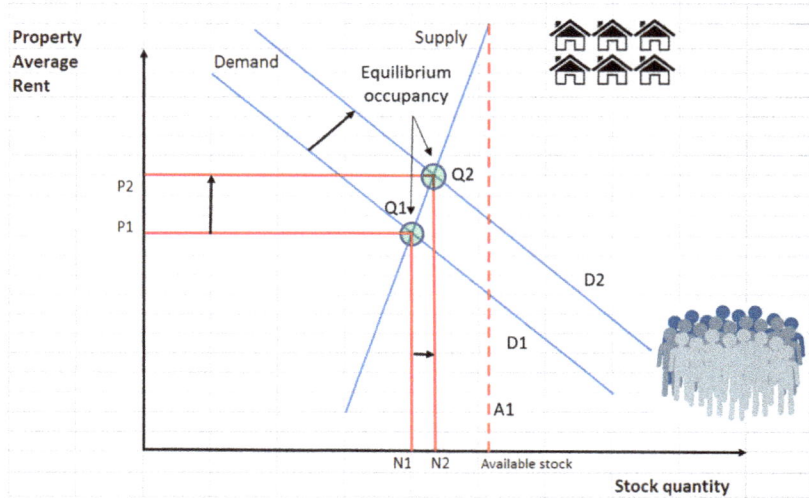

Figure 2.2 Rents increase due to higher demand

An increase in household real income is a demand shifter as well. When real income increases, individuals become more interested in buying better or bigger properties and are encouraged to move up the property ladder. This leads to a greater demand for housing and more competition amongst buyers, but a shortage of properties on the market. This causes the demand curve to shift to the right as well, as shown in figure 2.2, and results in a new equilibrium price P2 higher than previous value P1. Due to the inelasticity of supply, it would take time for developers to build new properties to meet the extra demand. This leads to an increase in property prices. When demand increases, it causes rents to increase to P2, sending a signal to investors that the rental market is progressing and something positive is happening.

Existing investors will try to expand their portfolios by developing new properties or remortgaging some of their existing properties. This allows them to raise funds to purchase more properties or to convert commercial properties to residential to meet demand. Also, new investors will try to enter the market, causing a further increase in the number of properties available i.e. from N2 to N3, as shown in figure 2.3. This additional demand drives up rent prices which affects the supply curve, causing it to shift from S1 to S2. Investors have reacted positively to the market demand and made use of the investment opportunity to supply the market with more properties, either by buying more BTLs or investing in a new development or conversion projects. However, a new equilibrium point Q3 is created by S2 at a price P3 which is a lower level than P2 due to increased supply by recent investments but still higher than P1.

Existing investors will try to expand their portfolios by developing new properties or remortgaging some of their existing properties. This allows them to raise funds to purchase more properties or to convert ccmmercial properties to residential to meet demand.

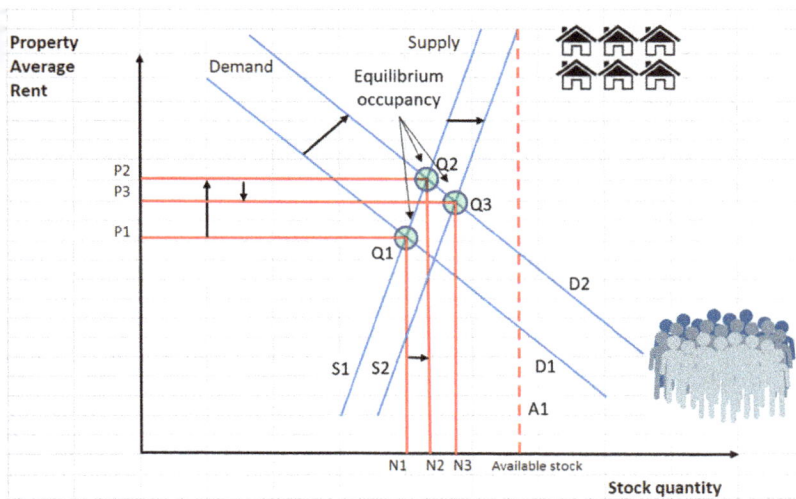

Figure 2.3 Due to increased demand more properties
were supplied by investors and developers

Property Pricing and Valuation

Property prices are determined by characteristics such as property structure (e.g. property design and size), location (e.g. distance to the central
business district (CBD)), neighbourhood (e.g. safety) and environment
(e.g. noise and air pollution). It is possible to determine a property price
for its structure and location but not its neighbourhood and other nearby
public "goods" or public "bads" which can be valued differently by buyers.
Property valuation is a different process that involves the assessment of
a property. There are a variety of factors used to value property such as
its size, age, condition, location etc. Surveyors often take care of such a
process and produce a valuation report with information about the valued
property.

The valuation of real estate is not a straightforward process and involves
many factors related to the property itself i.e. its features such as the number
of rooms, size of property etc, and external factors such as public services,
public goods or public bads. The prices for internal factors can be calculated
but external factors are difficult to calculate. Public goods such as parks,
safety, and clean air represent services that are often publicly financed,
accessible to all members of a community and do not diminish (non-
depletable) due to consumption by members of the community. A high
crime rate represents a public bad which is opposite to public good.

The property value is determined by the willingness of the buyer to pay
for both property-related features and external factors. However, we need to
compromise or try to achieve an equilibrium between different public goods
and public bads. For example, living closer to a CBD, you pay a premium
for city-style living and accept all the noise associated with it. The closer a
property is to a CBD, the higher the prices but the further the distance into
the countryside, the greater its beautiful views and calmness. Be aware that

> The property value
> is determined by the
> willingness of the buyer
> to pay for both proper-
> ty-related features and
> external factors.

public goods and public bads do not have a price and are not offered in the market. Here is a list of some public goods and public bads.
Public goods:

- Parks
- Countryside
- Safety e.g. crime control
- Quality infrastructure (e.g. streetlights, sewer system, motorway)
- Public schools and hospitals
- Libraries
- Clean air
- Free-to-air media: free tv or radio broadcasting

Public bads:

- Crime
- Noise
- Polluted air
- Flooding
- Landfill sites
- Poor infrastructure

We can use hedonic models to estimate prices of public goods, which can then contribute to the pricing process and become part of the property valuation. Hedonic models use statistical techniques to estimate the prices of certain non-marketable characteristics which can influence the valuation of properties. Many studies have analysed the characteristics and features of public goods and examined the effect of public goods on property values. The hedonic methodology has been used in the valuation of public goods and in investigating whether buyers are willing to pay more for accessible public goods. The positive impact of public goods and the negative impact of public bads on real estate have been studied widely and documented. It is possible to derive attributes and determine values for public goods and public bads using hedonic models.

The major challenges in using hedonic methodology are identifying all relevant factors and finding the necessary quantitative data for public goods or bads to model the hedonic system. Missing important variables and lack of data for some attributes could have a knock-on effect on the modelling results and consequently on property valuation. However, data such as physical housing characteristics and neighbourhood, purchase prices and transaction records, demographic data, schools' quality and ratings, and crime rates could be obtained from various government departments, national organisations, and private entities.

Property Tax

Governments try to resolve different issues and minimise the effect of various problems in society in general and the property sector in particular. Taxation is a powerful tool used by the government to resolve economic problems and to plan for the future. According to Danny Myers[3], the main

---

Hedonic models use statistical techniques to estimate the prices of certain non-marketable characteristics which can influence the valuation of properties.

problems that are facing the government in the property sector include but are not limited to:

- Increased demand and limited supply
- Unfair competition
- Pollution
- Increased property prices
- Shortage of skilled labour
- Green belt destruction

These problems represent external factors that create additional costs which were not considered by the developers or property investors. Such additional costs should be added to the original expenses of property development projects. To achieve that the government introduces different sorts of tax regimes such as stamp duty, Capital Gains Tax etc. to the property business and transactions to help support the efforts to resolve those problems, as shown in figure 2.4. Property-related tax does play a role in increasing property prices and development projects. Also, tax has implications for the real estate market as well as property supply and demand.

As a result of property tax, a new equilibrium point Q2 has been created with an increased price from P1 to P2. The introduced tax of an amount P2 − P1 might help in terms of resolving some of those previously identified problems. However, the tax has created new challenges for the government in terms of affordability and reduced supply from N1 to N2 due to increased property prices and development costs respectively. Reduced supply would lead to a reduction in the available stock and increased demand. Also, the maximum number of available stock for renting decreased from A1 to A2, as shown in figure 2.4.

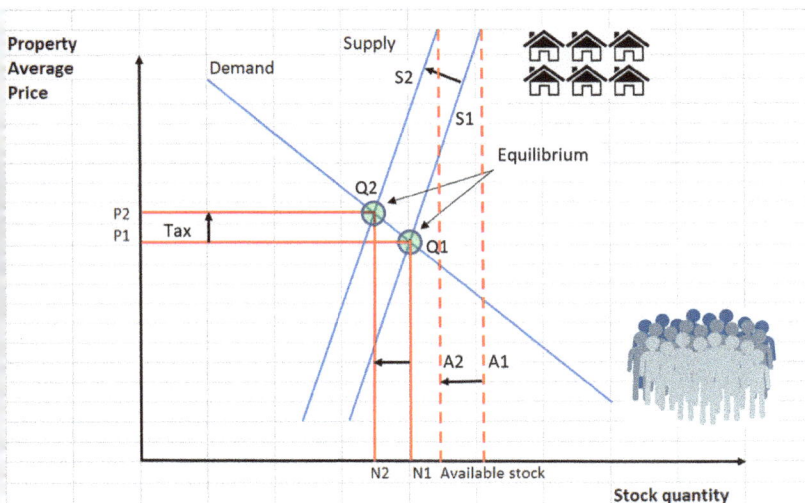

Figure 2.4 Tax implications on property price

In England and Wales, a recent property tax system has been introduced by the government. From 6 April 2020, BTL (buy-to-let) gross income (without a deduction for mortgage interest payments) will become taxable. This will result in an increased tax bill for many landlords. BTL Mortgage Interest

Tax Relief (MITR) for property mortgage costs will be limited to the basic 20% rate as a reduction in the rental tax bill. Running BTL expenses can still be deducted from gross rental income the same as before. Landlords with good rental cover (low mortgage costs relative to rental income) are less impacted. However, higher rate and additional rate taxpayers (40% and 45%) are highly impacted. Recently, many landlords have set up companies to manage their BTL property business and to minimise the costs associated with tax introduced by the government.

Summary

In this chapter, the relationship between supply and demand and their effects on real estate prices and economics has been introduced. Due to limited property stock and supply, the dynamics of the rental market determine the available housing for tenants and their demand. The shortage in housing stock represents an economic challenge to the UK government in terms of increased demand and sometimes inflated prices. Therefore, various topics related to real estate pricing, valuation, taxation and its implications on the markets as well as supply and demand have been presented. Due to the dynamic nature of the real estate markets, the next chapter presents the economic factors that can influence the real estate business. Economic factors such as interest rate, planning rules and regulations and their impact on supply and demand will be discussed in the following chapter. Investors need to be aware of inflation and how it affects mortgages, property prices, and buying power. The next chapter will also cover various issues related to funding real estate investment projects, as well as inflation and its impact on real estate investment and economics.

Bank and Government Interventions

3

As a dynamic market, the real estate business is influenced by supply and demand and other economic factors. Factors such as interest rates, local authorities' planning rules, government regulations, etc. play a role in causing shifts in the supply and demand curves and thus shifts in the market. Without money offered by banks, investors would not be able to fund and develop their investment projects. Issues regarding funding, investors, and governments will be covered first. Investors need to be aware of inflation and its impact on mortgages, savings, property prices, buying power, and the value of money over time. This chapter ends with a brief discussion about inflation and its impact on real estate investment and people in general.

Banks and Government

Money moves around the globe and the clock between individuals, organisations, financial institutions, and governments. Without funds offered by banks, investors and businesses would not be able to fund their investments or develop their projects. Banks compete amongst each other to increase their market share by attracting more customers and real estate businesses that need capital to grow. Banks invest the money deposited by their customers by selling financial products, mortgages, providing loans, lending to property investors or businesses, or buying and selling assets. They are allowed by the central bank to lend about 90% of deposited money to other customers. This helps banks to make money and boost the economy. Banks make money from real estate mortgages to help them pay for their operational costs and generate profits through various other enhanced service offerings such as:

> Without funds offered by banks, investors and businesses would not be able to fund their investments or develop their projects.

- Transaction charges
- Charging mortgage fees
- Interest on their mortgage products
- Redemption fees, and
- Overdraft penalties etc.

Governments use various options and financial tools to boost the economy and to minimise the effects of recession or depression, during which money supply is restricted. During a recession, the economy shrinks, trading activities and wages fall and unemployment rises. Due to the reduction in employment, people spend less and start to save which will have an impact on the economy in general and real estate in particular. A continued period of recession could lead to a more serious economic situation known as depression which is much worse than recession. To avoid that, governments tend to monitor the money supply in the economy especially during times of recession, and to adjust the cash reserves accordingly. This would allow them to make decisions on whether or not to inject more cash into the economy and increase money circulation. Governments use three options to finance their budget:

- Taxation such as CGT (Capital Gains Tax) and SDLT (Stamp Duty Land Tax)
- Borrowing money, and
- Printing more money through central banks

Real estate investors are expected to pay tax to the government from their business profits. When the government's collected revenues from tax are more than it is spending, it has a surplus. However, when the government's spending on its financial commitments exceeds income and additional funds are needed, it may have to borrow money or go for the risky option of printing money. The difference between the government's spending and its income is known as the budget deficit. The deficit determines how much extra money the government needs to borrow or print to pay for public spending and fulfil its financial commitments. In addition to money printing, governments can create electronic money but they need to be careful because increasing the money supply faster than economic growth will cause hyperinflation. Therefore, part of the central bank's job is to supply the required money and implement the government's monetary policies and meet its economic targets.

Many economists believe that extra spending and investment by governments is necessary to stimulate economic activities and to maintain a balanced market. By injecting more money into the economy, unemployment could be reduced due to increased demand for products and services. However, governments also tighten their spending when inflation rises due to prolonged growth rate and an overheated economy, as shown in figure 3.1. Both the government and central bank play a critical role in the supply of money, its circulation and spending in the country's economy. Central banks are in charge of monetary policy, managing the country's monetary system and responding to unpleasant economic situations, as shown in figure 3.2. This includes setting the exchange rate and base rate, currency, country's reserve and supply of money. All those measures have an impact on the property mortgages interest rate and property market.

> Both the government and central bank play a critical role in the supply of money, its circulation and spending in the country's economy.

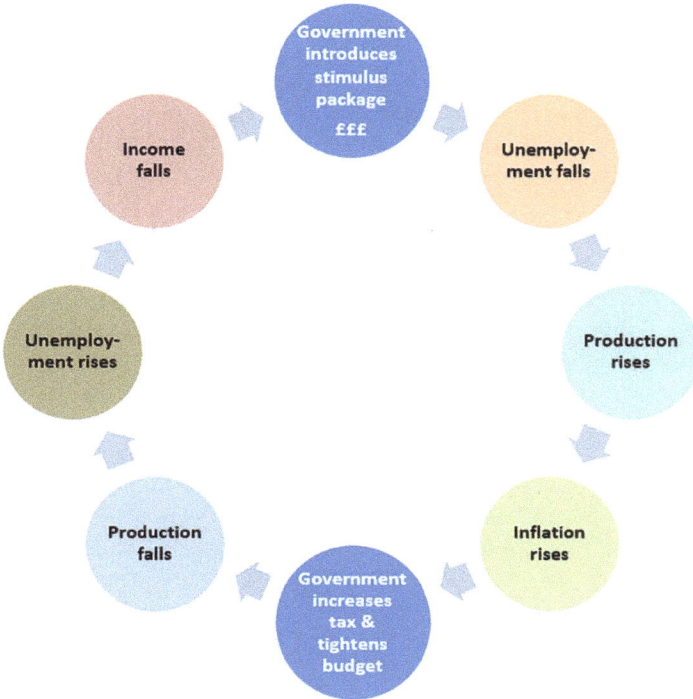

Figure 3.1 Economic cycle

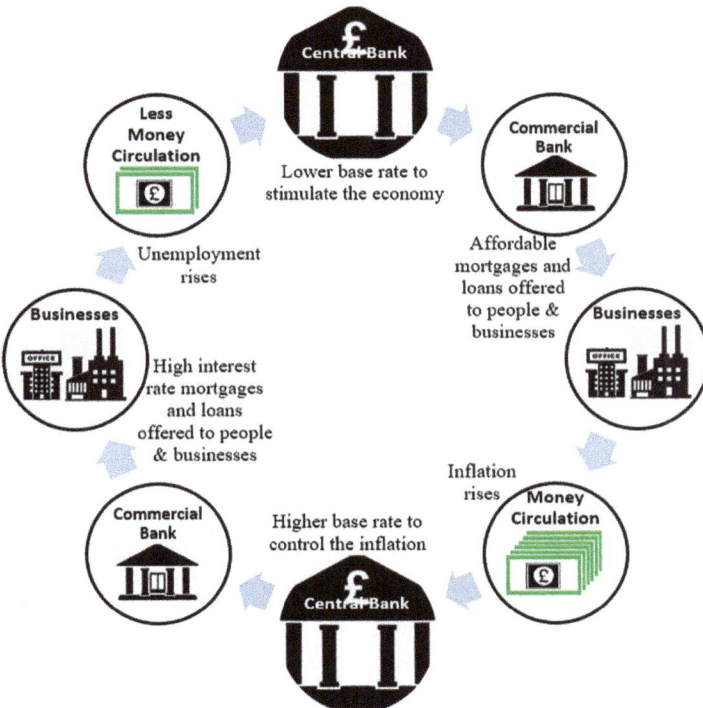

Figure 3.2 Central bank's response to recession and rise of inflation

Inflation

It is important to understand how inflation affects savings, real estate prices, and the value of money over time.

Inflation is a rise in price levels of goods and services over some time and a fall in buying power. It is associated with economic growth and control of money supply. It is important to understand how inflation affects savings, real estate prices, and the value of money over time. The CPI (Consumer Price Index) is a measure used to track inflation by monitoring the cost of goods and services. There are various factors such as rising property prices, oil or gold prices and labour costs that can have an impact on inflation. Also, supply and demand play a significant role in the inflation rate. Central banks can control inflation by raising and lowering short-term interest rates, as discussed in the previous section.

Let us see how the value of the dollar has changed over a specific period. Inflation analysis helps real estate investors to predict the amount they need in a certain time during inflation to keep the same buying and investment power. Figure 3.3 shows the change in the value of $1,000 over a long period, from 2000 to 2025. Also, the figure shows a projected inflation rate of 2.22% was used to calculate values from 2021 to 2025.

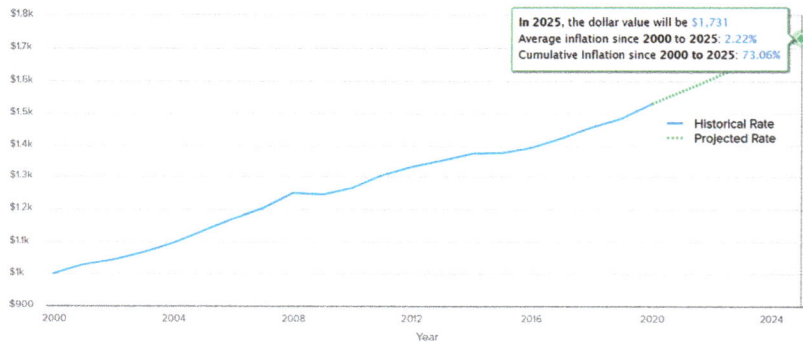

Figure 3.3 The change in the value of $1,000 from 2000 to 2025 – Source: https://smartasset.com/investing/inflation-calculator

Another factor that investors need to be aware of is the ROI (return on investment) which is a well-known metric used to measure the performance of a particular investment using a mathematical formula.

The average inflation of 2.22% is not bad as an initial $1,000 inflates by around 73% after 25 years. However, inflation could cause clear damage to people's savings and investment because of a minor increase of even 1% in the long run. Another factor that investors need to be aware of is the ROI (return on investment) which is a well-known metric used to measure the performance of a particular investment using a mathematical formula. It is used to evaluate the returned initial investment during a period. For example, it should take about 10 years to return an initial investment at 7.2% ROI with an inflation of 0%. However, investors should aim for a higher ROI if they want to double their money in less than 10 years, as shown in table 3.1 below.

Annualised ROI	No of years to return initial investment
2.8%	25
3.5%	20
4.7%	15
7.2%	10
10.4%	7
14.9%	5

Table 3.1 ROI calculations

We can compute the annual percentage return on investment using the following formula:

$$Annualised\ ROI = ((Principal + Gained\ Value) / Principal)^{1/n} - 1\ x\ 100$$

ROI must keep up with the inflation rate to improve the buying and investment power. For example, an inflation rate of 3% after an investment return of 2.8% will not produce a positive return (2.8% − 3% = -0.2%). Inflation can reduce the returns of an investment, which is why understanding inflation is important. Diversifying an investment business, for example with exposure to BTL (buy-to-let), HMO (Housing of Multiple Occupancy), or REITs may help investors protect their investment returns against inflation.

It is useful to determine how much money can grow using the power of compound interest in comparison to ROI. Compounding interest includes all of the accumulated interest from several years on an investment or savings. It grows at a faster rate than simple interest, boosts investment returns, and makes a significant difference to the initial investment over the long term, as shown in table 3.2. Figure 3.4 below shows approximate figures for how much an initial saving will grow over time for different scenarios. It highlights the results of doubling initial investment of $10,000 savings using interest of 10.4% in 7 years. Be aware that inflation compounds like interest as well.

> Diversifying an investment business, for example with exposure to BTL (buy-to-let), HMO (Housing of Multiple Occupancy), or REITs may help investors protect their investment returns against inflation.

Interest rate per year	No of years to return initial investment
2.8%	25
3.5%	20
4.7%	15
7.2%	10
10.4%	7
14.9%	5

Table 3.2 Compound interest over a number of years

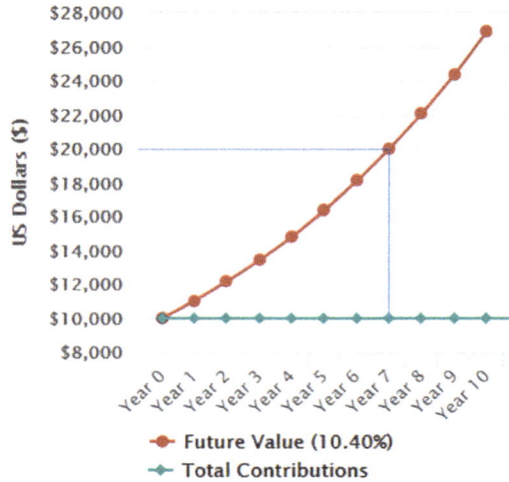

Figure 3.4 Doubling initial investment of $10,000 savings in 7 years using 10.4% compound interest – Adapted from https://www.investor.gov/[4]

The compound interest can be calculated using the following formula:

$$= P \left[(1 + i)^n - 1 \right]$$

Where P = initial principal or initial investment or saving amount,
i = nominal annual interest rate, and
n = number of compounding periods

Real Estate Investment and Economy

Real estate investment plays a major role in the economy of any society and in promoting its development. It is an important element in attracting foreign investment, supporting various industries, improving employment rates and production, and providing significant growth to local communities and the national economy. Therefore, we need to understand the relationship between real estate and all related industries, especially the interacting factors and linkages between them. The German economist Albert Hirschman[5] introduced the term "linkage" to describe the link between industries to emphasise the importance of connectivity between related industries. The expansion of real estate investment implies an increased demand for many industries and services to run and maintain those income-producing properties, creating an interesting network of interactions between all those industries. Figure 3.5 illustrates the interaction between residential investment property and other industries and service providers. It shows that real estate investment helps various industries to grow. For example, a real estate investment helps

> The expansion of real estate investment implies an increased demand for many industries and services to run and maintain those income-producing properties, creating an interesting network of interactions between all those industries.

- The insurance sector by paying building insurance
- The building supplies sector by developing refurbishment projects
- Local authorities by the payment of council tax through ensuring that vacant properties become occupied

- The government through payment of Capital Gains Tax, SDLT (Stamp Duty Land Tax), and income tax by real estate investors when buying, selling, and generating income from properties
- Certified electricians and plumbers through paying them to provide electric and gas safety checks and certificates, and so on

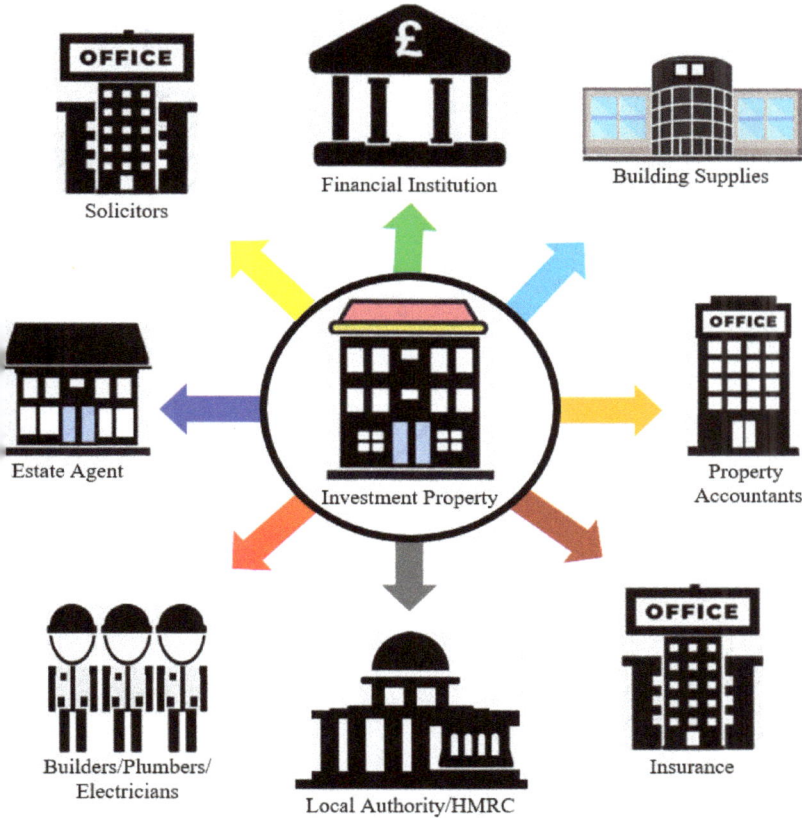

OFFICE

Solicitors

Financial Institution

Building Supplies

Estate Agent

OFFICE

Property Accountants

Investment Property

Builders/Plumbers/ Electricians

Local Authority/HMRC

OFFICE

Insurance

Figure 3.5 The interaction between an investment property and different industries and service providers

In the UK, average house prices are increasing at an accelerating rate, seeing growth in most regions, and residential property sales are continuing to grow. This includes the real estate development sector which continues to rise. Changes in real estate investment strategies can have an impact not only on property investors and tenants but also on many sectors such as building supplies, retailers, insurance, and banking.

The real estate investment sector makes a significant contribution to the financial sector and taxation system. This is because of the real estate businesses' influential factors such as supply and demand. Besides their substantial lending schemes, banks consider real estate as a guarantee for financing and their growth. However, alternative financing solutions and products from non-high street banks and crowdfunding have become more useful for investment projects. Figure 3.6 shows the quarterly changes in total secured lending to individuals between March 2012 and September

Besides their substantial lending schemes, banks consider real estate as a guarantee for financing and their growth.

2020. The fallen lending amount between March 2020 and September 2020 was due to the COVID-19 pandemic which had an impact on the real estate market and the economy as a whole.

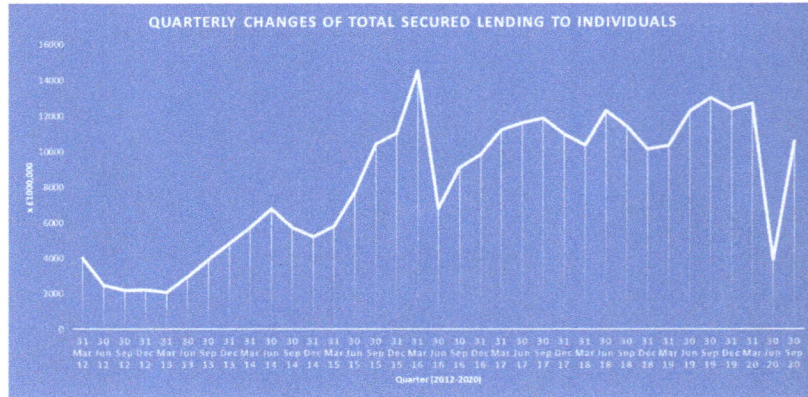

Figure 3.6 Changes in secured lending – Created using data from the Bank of England website[6]

Summary

The real estate business is influenced by various economic factors such as interest rates, local authorities' planning rules, government regulations, etc. as well as supply and demand. These factors can cause shifts in the supply and demand curves and thus shifts in the market. This chapter discussed how money offered by banks to investors would allow them to fund and develop their investment projects and improve property supply and market conditions. The issue of inflation and how it affects real estate investment has been introduced as well. Due to the importance of inflation, investors need to be aware of its impact on property prices, mortgages, and the value of money over time. This should help them analyse and assess the real estate market and make the right investment decisions. The next chapter covers the principles of market assessment, its methods, procedures, and its importance to gaining a proper understanding of the property business and planning. It presents a modified version of Porter's Five Forces model which has been developed to support property investors in their evaluation activities. Due to the importance of identifying the necessary resources to carry out a market assessment, the next chapter also provides useful information about real estate publishing organisations and content producers.

Assessing the Market

4

Market assessment helps investors gain a good understanding of the real estate market before making decisions and planning their strategies. Assessing and analysing the property market provides an overall picture of the market in terms of challenges and available opportunities. I have developed a modified version of Porter's Five Forces model to help investors evaluate the dynamic real estate industry. This chapter introduces the concepts and principles of real estate market assessment methods and procedures. Market assessment depends on the quality of the information and resources gathered. Therefore, investors have to gain the necessary skills of information gathering, research, and using the relevant technologies and tools to their advantage.

This chapter introduces the four main methods of information gathering which are interviews, networking, market observations, and research. Investors need to identify useful sources of information and material. This chapter also dedicates a section to information resources in terms of publishing organisations and content producers. The market assessment helps investors to evaluate the housing market in terms of supply and demand as well as market growth. The issues surrounding the housing market in the UK and its growth are presented at the end of the chapter.

Market Assessment

Investors need to dedicate time to carrying out market assessment and analysis before making any investment decision. This is necessary to understand the market, analyse data, and to check whether or not the market is suitable for investment. Investors need to make sure that the market provides opportunities and that their investment will be successful. A broader understanding of the market as a whole can illuminate certain opportunities and help with planning good business strategies. Also, it can help you develop an overall picture of the market and to check if resources and business abilities can meet the market challenges and requirements. Figure 4.1 shows a modified version of Porter's Five Forces model of Business Competition Analysis which was developed by Michael Porter of Harvard Business School in 1980[7].

Porter's model is a simple solution for market assessment and evaluation that can be used by a business organisation and/or investor. The model was introduced to identify the five main competitive forces that can help businesses in understanding the factors affecting profitability. The model has been modified to help business investors to determine the market challenges and the dynamic/changing characteristics of the real estate industry. Porter's Five Forces model is used to understand and

> A broader understanding of the market as a whole can illuminate certain opportunities and help with planning good business strategies.

analyse the level of competition within the property market and to develop a competitive strategy. I updated Porter's Five Forces model, as follows:

1. **Power of property suppliers:** To assess how easy it is for property developers or estate agents to raise prices. This depends on the level of property supply in terms of its size, the cost of new developments and the price of land as well as the number of properties for sale offered by estate agents or motivated sellers. The higher the number of property-for-sale options available to investors, the easier it is to find good deals.

2. **Power of tenants or buyers:** To assess how easy it is for tenants or property buyers to find alternatives and to drive prices down. Basically, investors should be able to assess how powerful they are. This depends on the number of properties available for rent or sale as well as the intensity of demand. Also, it depends on how flexible investors can be on the service they provide while maintaining an authoritative and attractive position in their market. They may consider targeting a specific type of tenant e.g. professionals or communities, or consider changing strategy if necessary.

3. **The threat of new entrants:** To assess the extent to which new, entrant investors are attracted to the property market and the extent to which experienced investors are surrounded by new competitors. The property market is tightly regulated and needs large amounts of investment capital with high financial risk. This makes it a challenging and competitive market for new starters, copycat businesses, and low-profile investors.

4. **The threat of substitutes:** To assess the ability of substitute accommodation service providers to introduce housing options to the market and how easy it is for renters to find an alternative to a property investor's service. This allows tenants and/or buyers to easily find alternatives in response to an increase in rents and/or property prices. This will have an impact on investors' income and/or profitability. Therefore, they may consider improving their level of service quality, offering a new service, changing strategy, or targeting a different market.

5. **Competition in the industry:** To assess the number and capabilities of investors, estate agents, and/or property developers in the market. The more capable competitors are chasing property deals and competing amongst each other, the less attractive the market is and the less power investors will have to stay competitive. In this case, they may consider identifying the strengths and limitations of their competitors and then develop a new strategy to stay resilient or become more competitive.

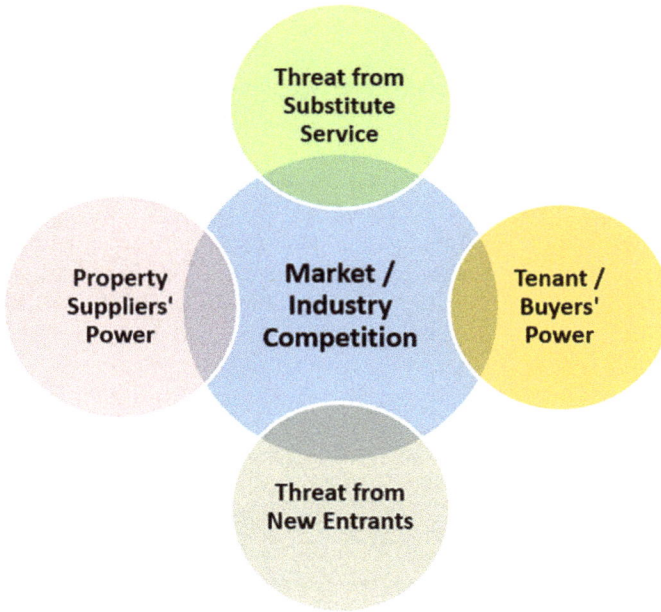

Figure 4.1 Real estate market assessment model
– Adapted from Porter's Five Forces[8]

A proper assessment of the market should help investors to find answers to the questions introduced in Porter's model and subsequently make better investment decisions. Evaluating the supply and demand should help investors to make sure that the demand for their accommodation service or strategy type is real. Understanding the target customers and their specific needs is very important in the investment business. Assessing the market, understanding the level of competition, and evaluating the level of service provided by competitors is an endless game.

Be aware, not all property business opportunities and strategies are worth pursuing unless they meet market conditions and customer needs. Selecting business options with the highest growth potential would be highly likely to lead to a successful investment. It is useful to identify the main market environment factors which can have a positive impact on investment strategic planning, business operations development, and competitive intelligence. The following list introduces the main market environment factors, which include but are not limited to:

- Employability rate
- Local authority regulations
- Infrastructure
- Transportation links
- Local amenities
- Demographic shifts
- Economic indicators

> Evaluating the supply and demand should help investors to make sure that the demand for their accommodation service or strategy type is real.

Information Gathering

Information is a key factor in any real estate investment, which must begin with a clear understanding of the market assessment and needs. It is important to be well resourced, whether it is with skills, technology, or material that can bring about progress and effective development. Information gathering is an important step in market research for quality data and information about the targeted area of investment. It is the beginning stage of market assessment, where the investor carries out the necessary information intelligence. The more information is collected about the targeted area, the more likely that relevant and useful results will be obtained. It is an art that every investor should master to gain the necessary knowledge and experience.

The information-gathering strategy would evolve through the investor collecting the relevant information at each stage of the investment. An investor's strategy should focus on identifying the main resources and obtaining necessary information from valid and recognised sources. There are various resources, techniques, and tools that are available for investors and can help them to collect vital information. There is no doubt it is a necessary step due to it being the critical stage of market assessment. The type of information that investors may need to gather includes but is not limited to:

- Average property prices
- Predicted market growth
- Expected yield
- Expected ROI
- Level of demand and supply
- Market strengths and weaknesses
- Market opportunities and threats
- The best strategy to use

To determine the requirements of investment, information must be gathered from the right sources. The information obtained will enable an investor to analyse well-defined facts and figures, and observe a complete picture of how the market operates as well as the entities and data involved. The type of information an investor is trying to obtain, and the entities providing the information, will determine which resources they should use. Many techniques can be employed when gathering information. Electronic information can be accessed online using the internet from any location or using other means of electronic communication. However, non-electronic information can only be accessed in person or through a face-to-face gathering at a certain location. Figure 4.2 shows the main methods used for information gathering. The four methods of gathering real estate investment information are:

- Interviews with local estate agents and letting agents
- Networking with peer investors during property network meetings e.g. PIN (Property Investor Network) meetings, conferences, seminars etc.
- Observation of the local market using local news and/or local authority online resources and published reports
- A research study of the existing market and published documents such as online resources, property magazines, and reports

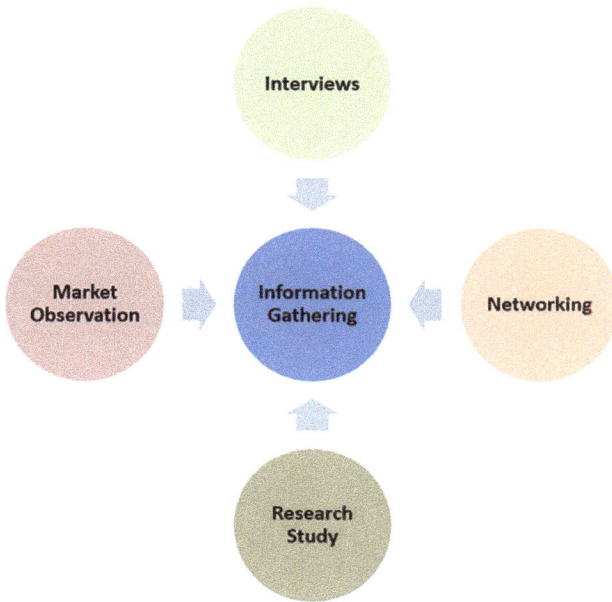

Figure 4.2 The main methods of information gathering

Information Resources

A variety of valuable information is produced by many useful publishing organisations. A lot of useful material has been published to provide quality content and information to property investors. This material enables access to significant and relevant data as well as information that can be used by investors to analyse the market and make investment decisions. Property information flows through various organisations and content producers such as NRLA (National Residential Landlord Association), ONS (Office of National Statistics), and publications such as property magazines, reports, books, etc. The following table 4.1 introduces a sample of information resources for real estate businesses in general and UK investors in particular.

> A lot of useful material has been published to provide quality content and information to property investors.

Information Type	Information Resource	Remarks
Magazines	**N RLA** Property Magazine	Looks into how to run private rental businesses
	property aspects MAGAZINE	Features a range of property issues within the UK
	LANDLORD INVESTOR LI MAGAZINE	Covers various areas of the buy-to-let market and private rented sector
News	**Property**notify	Provides news about leading property sector
	PropertyInvestorTODAY	Provides news about the property sector at the national level and overseas
	Homes&Property	Offers news about luxury property sales, mortgages, and guides
Organisations	**N RLA** NATIONAL RESIDENTIAL LANDLORDS ASSOCIATION	Provides support to the property business community in terms of training, documents, and guides
	LANDLORD ACTION	Offers support to landlords in terms of eviction, debt recovery and legal matters
	Investopedia	An online publisher that provides financial news and advice as well as educational material about the investment

Information Type	Information Resource	Remarks
Government bodies	Ministry of Housing, Communities & Local Government	Provides guides to landlords and info about housing and local services
	NATIONAL STATISTICS	Provides statistics and dataset related to the construction industry and real estate activities in the UK
	HM Revenue & Customs	Provides services and information about money, tax, and housing
Media	BBC NEWS Housing market	Publishes news about the housing market
	itv NEWS Property	Publishes news about the property market
	property reporter	Reports news about the property business
Shows and exhibitions	NATIONAL LANDLORD INVESTMENT SHOW	UK leading landlord and property investment exhibition
	THE LUXURY PROPERTY SHOW	Europe's leading luxury property show

Table 4.1 Information resources for real estate businesses

The collection of information on market analytical figures and reports is a time consuming and labour intensive process. This requires a lot of research skills and knowledge of information analysis. There are many cost-effective resources available for property investors to help them find the information they need to better assess the housing market. These resources should help investors to gain the necessary knowledge from recent reports, and understand the business environment and current property demand and supply. They are:

There are many cost-effective resources available for property investors to help them find the information they need to better assess the housing market.

- Land Registry
  - https://landregistry.data.gov.uk/
  - https://www.gov.uk/government/organisations/land-registry

- UK House Price Index Reports
  - The UK HPI provides information about changes in the value of residential properties in the UK.
  - https://www.gov.uk/government/collections/uk-house-price-index-reports

- The Royal Institution of Chartered Surveyors (RICS)
  - RICS is a recognised organisation that operates at the highest professional standards to influence policy and to publish reports. RICS is a regulatory body that actively monitors the development and management of land, real estate, construction, and infrastructure.
  - https://www.rics.org/uk/

- Estate agents, letting agents, sourcing agents, investor networks

- Online resources
  - e.g. rightmove.co.uk, zoopla.co.uk
  - Rightmove is one of the largest property portals that is used for advertising, searching, and researching properties. Their online property search platform provides information about properties for sale, their prices, and locations. It is used by estate agents and letting agents to advertise their properties for sale and rent respectively. Rightmove focuses on the UK property advertising market and seeks to reach UK property advertisers. Figure 4.3 shows search results of properties for sale for prices equal to or more than £350,000 in the greater Manchester area.

- Auctions
  - e.g. https://www.eigpropertyauctions.co.uk/
  - EIG is an online portal that provides information on virtually every property advertised for sale through auction and those offered in the past. As a property business resource, EIG focuses on UK property auctions.

- Church and police commissions[9]
  - They manage their organisations' property portfolios and use estate agents or auctions to sell their properties. For example, about twenty church properties that are suitable for use are offered for sale every year.

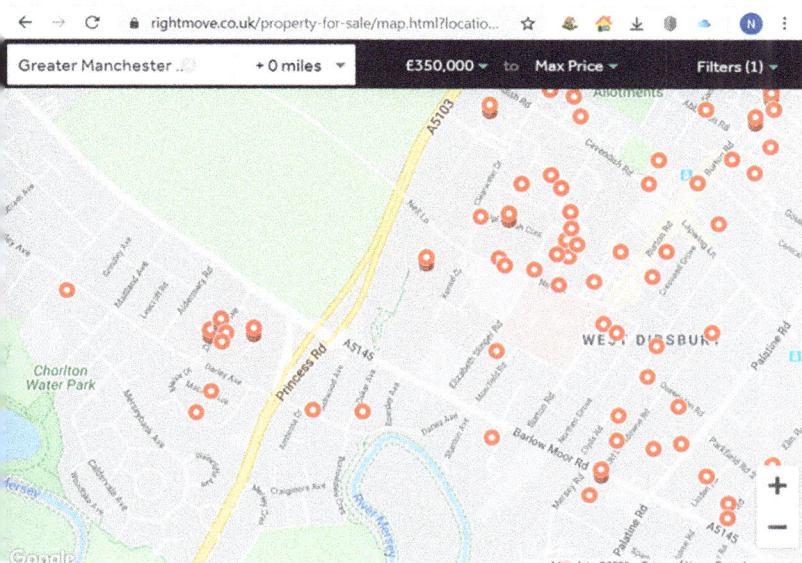

Figure 4.3 Search results of properties for sale – Source: rightmove.co.uk portal

Housing Market

In the UK, the number of new households each year has exceeded the number of homes built every year since 2008, and the need for additional housing in England stands at ~ 232,000 to 300,000 new units per year, a level of demand that has not been reached since the 1970s and two to three times the current supply (www.parliament.uk)[10]. According to the Office for National Statistics (ONS)[11] in the UK, the average UK house price was £234,000 in September 2019, with the average in England £251,000, in Wales £164,000, Scotland £155,000 and Northern Ireland £140,000. In 2019, the North West of England had the highest annual house price growth, with prices increasing by 2.8%, followed by Yorkshire and the Humber, increasing by 2.2%.

The lowest annual house price growth was in London, where prices dropped by 0.4% over the year to September 2019. The other region that had negative annual growth was the East of England, where prices dropped by 0.2% over the year, as shown in figure 4.4. London remains the most expensive region to purchase a property at an average of £475,000 despite the continued house price fall over the year. Due to limited economic growth, the North East continued to have the lowest average house price at £133,000, as shown in figure 4.5.

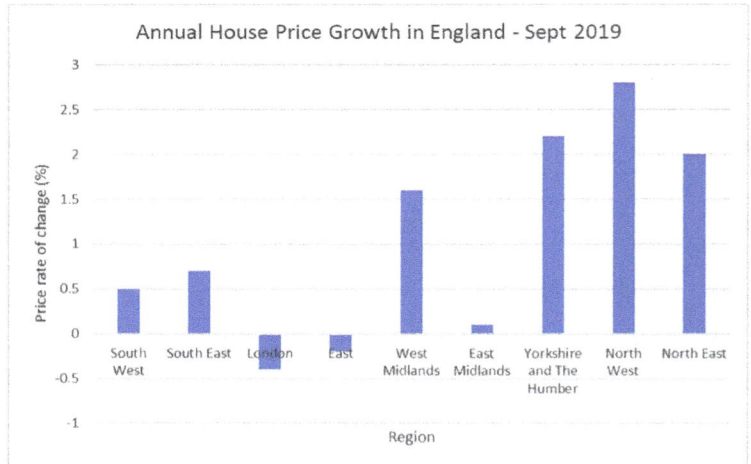

Figure 4.4 Annual house price growth in England, Sept 2019 –
Created using data from the Office for National Statistics[12]

It is important to evaluate the housing market in terms of average house prices, level of growth, and intensity of supply and demand, and to check if there is room for growth. Investors need to ask themselves some of these questions:

- What is the current supply and demand?
- What is the size of the market?
- What is the likelihood of market growth?
- What is the intensity of competition and who are the current competitors?
- What is the best strategy to use?
- What are the main challenges and barriers to entry?
- What are the main opportunities and threats?

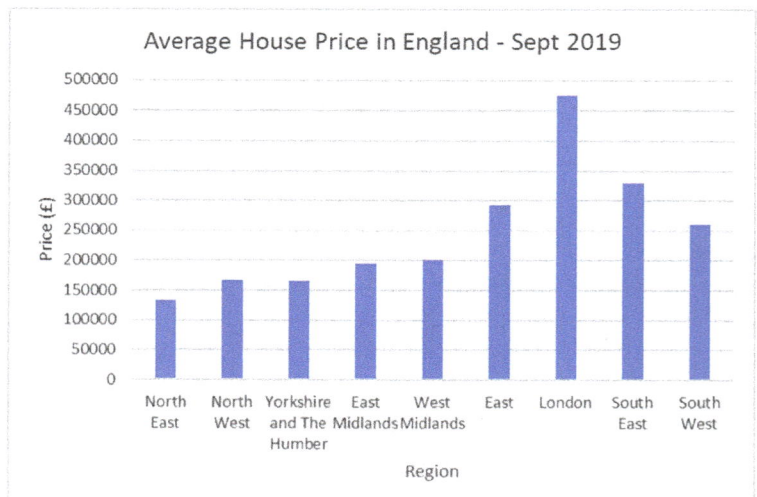

Figure 4.5 Average house price in England, Sept 2019 –
Adapted from the Office for National Statistics[13]

Summary

Investors need to understand how to assess the property market to gain a good understanding of it as well as its challenges and opportunities, and make proper investment decisions. This chapter provided useful information including the general concepts and principles of market assessment which can help investors to gain the necessary skills and knowledge to carry out their investment activities. A modified version of Porter's Five Forces model was presented to support investors in carrying out their market assessment and evaluation. This chapter also introduced the four main methods of information gathering which investors need to identify useful resources. These will help them not only to identify publishing organisations and content producers but also to implement their own investment strategies. The next chapter will introduce real estate investment and how investors can put their capital into income-producing properties. It will also describe the different asset classes which can offer multiple streams of income and/or capital gains. In addition, real estate business philosophy and how the UK government deals with this industry will be discussed. Finally it will consider the main types of residential and commercial properties alongside information about real estate prices and the main skills required by investors.

An Introduction to Real Estate Investment

5

Real estate investment is about putting capital into an asset to produce a return. This can include the use of different asset classes which offer different types of return such as monthly rental income, capital gains, or dividends from REITs (Real Estate Investment Trusts) stocks. However, before making an investment decision, investors need to assess the market as well as their financial situation. This chapter aims to introduce the subject of real estate investment, cover aspects of real estate business and philosophy, and discuss how the UK government deals with this industry in terms of regulations and financial implications. The main types of residential and commercial properties are also introduced, alongside general information about property prices in various regions in the UK. Property investors need to be aware of the various qualities and abilities they need to establish a successful real estate business, therefore the main skills and knowledge required to get into property investment are also presented at the end of this chapter.

Real Estate Business and Philosophy

The real estate business has attracted both local and international investors to invest in the UK property market. Because of this, real estate investment has created billions of pounds' worth of property transactions every year by property investors. These investors have managed to build up a stock of profitable properties and create successful investment portfolios. Investors tend to think about their investment philosophy when determining their approach to investing. As an investor of many years, my philosophy is to acquire assets of high demand which produce high returns with manageable risks to meet my financial goals, as shown in figure 5.1. In other words, to buy properties in good locations where there is a clear demand, generate passive income and high yield, and achieve financial independence.

Investors' philosophy reflects their way of thinking about investment and belief in their financial goals. However, their investment strategy is an activity that requires them to make effective decisions and utilise available resources to manage their investment operations. Before starting their real estate business journey and making decisions on their investment, investors need to have a proper understanding of the differences between the two main types of real estate – residential and commercial. This allows them to

Investors' philosophy reflects their way of thinking about investment and belief in their financial goals.

narrow their investment options based on what they are interested in and what they are capable of.

"Your time is limited, so don't waste it living someone else's life. Don't be trapped by dogma which is living with the results of other people's thinking. Don't let the noise of others' opinions drown out your own inner voice. And most important, have the courage to follow your heart and intuition. They somehow already know what you truly want to become. Everything else is secondary."

Steve Jobs

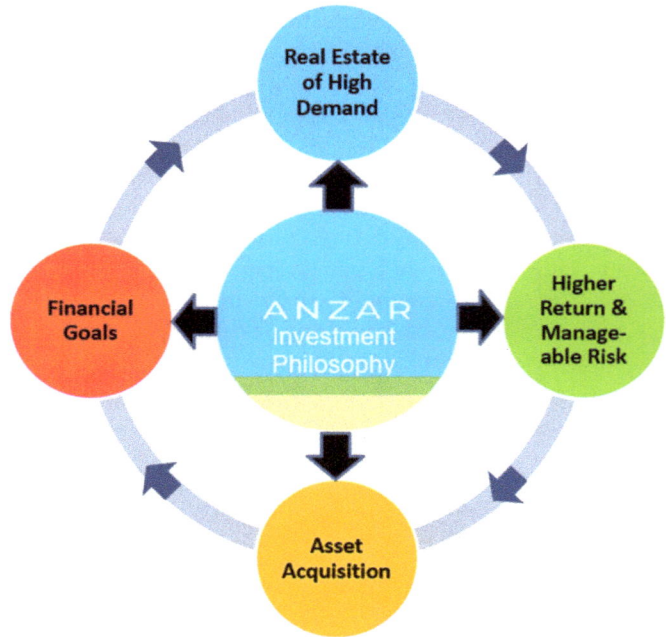

Figure 5.1 My investment philosophy

Each type of property investment has its characteristics, advantages, and drawbacks. Residential and commercial properties vary in almost every way in terms of occupancy, usage, design, leasing contracts, and funding. While commercial properties will have wide functionality and are often developed for general uses, the functionality of residential properties can be limited and developed for specific uses. Due to their extensive functionality, commercial properties require more focus and attention. There will be excessive need for certain services such as security, lifts, lighting, storage, server rooms, etc. Also, commercial investment tends to provide investors with a much wider range of potential opportunities such as higher yield and more funding products and options.

Residential and commercial properties vary in almost every way in terms of occupancy, usage, design, leasing contracts, and funding.

*"Rule number 1, never lose money. Rule number 2, never forget
rule number 1. Price is what you pay. Value is what you get."*
Warren Buffett

*"Real estate cannot be lost or stolen, nor can it be carried away.
Purchased with common sense, paid for in full, and managed with
reasonable care, it is about the safest investment in the world."*
Franklin D. Roosevelt

Real Estate Investment and UK Government

The UK government uses property tax such as stamp duty, Capital Gains Tax, etc. to help and support the efforts towards funding its national projects and resolving various economic problems. Like many countries, the UK's economy relies heavily on the property market; tens of billions of overseas investments generate income for the government through a tax which helps manage the country's deficit. Changes in property prices or tax might not only affect property business cashflows and investments, but also the country's economy, its credit rating, and GDP. Recently, the UK government has introduced property tax changes to MITR (Mortgage Interest Tax Relief) which have resulted in an increased tax bill for many BTL (buy-to-let) landlords and investors. The new tax measures introduced by the Conservative government are not meant to restrict BTL investments because the property business plays a major role in the growth of the UK economy. However, it seems that the purpose of the introduced tax system is not only to collect more tax which is important, but also to minimise the losses of unpaid tax from private landlords.

> Changes in property prices or tax might not only affect property business cashflows and investments, but also the country's economy, its credit rating, and GDP.

The UK government has failed to meet its targets of annual property supply since the 1990s. But the government is trying to slow down the growth of property prices especially in London and the South East and give first-time buyers a chance to get on the property ladder. Also, it seems the reason behind the new tax system was to professionalise the BTL business and force low-profile landlords with just a few BTL properties to either become professional by setting up property limited companies or be replaced by those who are serious and are willing to incorporate. Limited companies only pay Corporation Tax on their annual profits. This new tax system has forced many landlords to abandon the BTL business in favour of company owners. There are challenges and tax obligations to transfer ownership of BTL properties to a company but there are legal ways to minimise such costs.

> Limited companies only pay Corporation Tax on their annual profits.

According to bid rent theory, rent price and demand for properties tend to increase as the distance from the CBD (central business district) decreases. However, sustainable buildings are expected to achieve a substantial rise in rental prices in the future, especially if they are located within the CBD. The UK government encourages the development of green buildings by offering various financial support schemes, such as property tax assessment incentives, environmental tax schemes, RHI (Renewable Heat Incentive), and green financial products known as green mortgages. Therefore, investors are expected to achieve a higher net operating income due to lower operating expenses and cost-effective financial products. Something to seriously consider for future investments!

Types of Real Estate Properties

There are different types of real estate that can be used to generate rental income. Real estate can be divided into two main categories, residential and commercial. Residential properties are exclusively used as a dwelling to offer accommodation, often located in areas where housing predominates, and can be used as income-producing real estate. They refer to buildings that are designed to be occupied by individuals, single families, or multiple families. Multi-family housing includes apartment buildings, condominiums, and skyscrapers. Such buildings are used to house many families and share green space and some services among themselves. There are numerous types of residential properties built with a variety of different designs, architectural styles, and building structures. Figure 5.2 shows the average price by property type in the UK during February 2020. The main types of residential properties are shown below:

There are numerous types of residential properties built with a variety of different designs, architectural styles, and building structures.

Main types of residential properties	
Detached homes	
Semi-detached	
Terraced	
Townhouse	
Maisonette	
Apartment buildings	
Condominiums	
Bungalow	
Skyscraper	

Table 5.1 Types of residential properties

Average Price by Property Type in the UK - Feb 2020

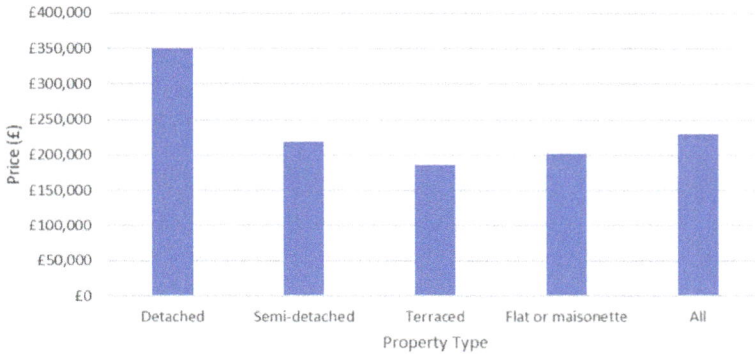

Figure 5.2 Average price by property type in the UK, Feb 2020 – Adapted from UK HPI (House Price Index[14])

Condominiums and skyscrapers are good examples of property investments with mixed use. They are multi-storey buildings that combine different types of properties and offer multiple services and shared areas such as green space and playgrounds for children. Such properties may contain residential flats, hotels, retail markets, fitness facilities, swimming pools, and/or business offices. The major difference between both of them is that condominiums may contain detached buildings or blocks of flats but skyscrapers are supertall buildings and often located inside CBDs like Beetham Tower and Deansgate Square towers (North, South, East, and West) in Manchester city centre.

Commercial properties refer to buildings or premises that are designed to provide workspace and house businesses. They are business-focused and used by tenants to carry out commercial activities and to generate a profit such as shops, supermarkets, banks, offices, and/or shopping centres, etc. The performance of commercial properties in terms of their produced income, business activities, and occupancy rate play a major role in their valuation and price indices. As with residential properties, investors in commercial properties can aim for capital appreciation. The rental returns from commercial buildings are often higher than those from residential properties. Commercial properties are less sophisticated and provide better control over the lease terms. Also, commercial properties are less labour intensive in terms of managing tenants and building maintenance. They are traded publicly in REITs (Real Estate Investment Trusts) which provide an opportunity for investors to indirectly invest in commercial real estate. There are five different types of commercial buildings as shown overleaf:

The performance of commercial properties in terms of their produced income, business activities, and occupancy rate play a major role in their valuation and price indices.

No	Commercial Property	Tenants / Business	
1	Office buildings	Accountants, lawyers, dentists	
2	Hotel	Tourists, travellers, temporary workforce	
3	Retail space	Shopping centres, malls, retail parks	
4	Industrial buildings	Factories, warehouses, storage units, research and development (R&D)	
5	Institutional buildings	Hospitals, banks, clubs, local authorities, universities, government	

Table 5.2 Types of commercial buildings

To consider investing in real estate, a proper market analysis is required to determine the level of supply and demand in the area. Figure 5.3 shows the sale volumes by country in the UK in December 2019; such information is important for investment analysis. It is useful to gather information about the factors that influence supply and demand for certain areas and different types of properties. Investors also need detailed information about:

- Level of occupancy
- Current and/or new development projects
- Job markets
- Average household salaries
- Available infrastructure
- Local amenities
- Location
- Demographic changes
- Type of properties desired by local communities

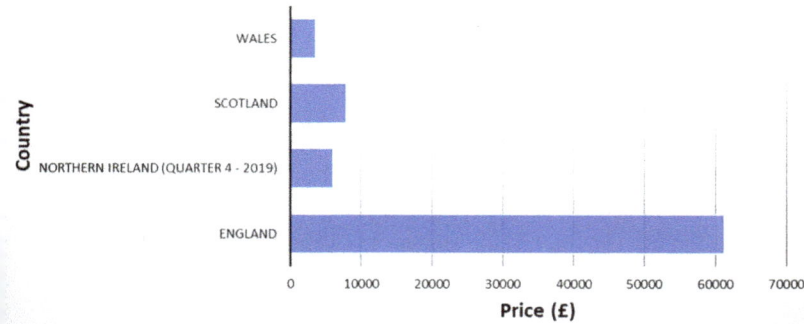

Figure 5.3 Number of sales volumes by country, Dec 2019 – Adapted from UK HPI (House Price Index)[15]

Another aspect that investors need to consider when they invest in the UK market is that if they buy a freehold property, they own the land as well, so they won't pay ground rent. On the other hand, if they own a leasehold property, they will have to pay ground rent to the freeholder. If the lease period is a few hundred years then it is fine. However, banks in the UK don't lend for properties which have a lease period of less than 70 years. It is possible to buy the freehold if the offered price by the freeholder is within the investor's budget and if it is worth the investment. In the UK, almost all flats are sold as leasehold.

Real Estate Investors

Investors should have the capability to carry out a proper study and detailed analysis of their targeted area for investment. The outcome of their study and analysis in terms of supply and demand should help them in terms of identifying the positives and negatives before making their investment decisions. The supply of properties in the market tends to take time to complete and it requires an even longer time to effectively adapt to an increase in demand. Unlike other businesses, property investment is a long-term business with long economic life, requiring long-term vision, large amounts of capital, and access to a large number of funds. Therefore, active investors who are actively involved in investment operations are not reluctant to take a risk, manage and deal with lots of capital, and invest in their business projects.

Active investors take the risk of starting up their companies, investing time to gain the "know-how" knowledge to deal with various entities such as banks, solicitors, local authorities, insurers, etc. They are willing to interact with all the stakeholders and deal with all aspects of the business in terms of marketing, sales, technology, real estate economics, finance, accounting, operations management, strategic planning, etc. All these activities are important to the real estate business and require certain qualities and skills to build a successful investment. That is why investors are risk-takers and that's what makes them different to the majority, as shown in figure 5.4.

> Unlike other businesses, property investment is a long-term business with long economic life, requiring long-term vision, large amounts of capital, and access to a large number of funds.

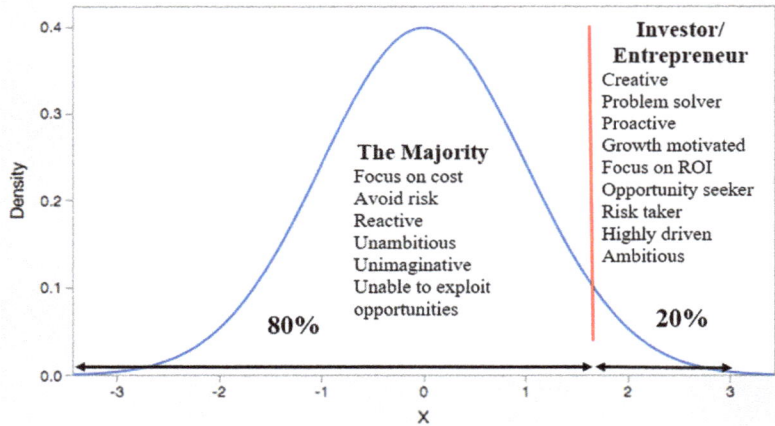

Figure 5.4 Investors and the majority – Adapted from the Pareto Principle (80/20 Rule)[16]

Investors would be expected to deal with high street and non-high street banks to get lending and fund their investment projects. Lenders offer various mortgage options, fixed and variable rates using mortgage terms, often two, three or five years. If an investor decides to pay their mortgage in full through remortgaging before the end of their mortgage term, they would expect to pay an early payment penalty, also known as an early redemption fee. Investors may decide to do so when refinancing any of their properties before the end of the mortgage term. This usually occurs after the investor has added value to a property and is confident the refinance will be successful. This enables the investor to get access to extra funds, despite the unpleasant cost of early payment penalties, which are part of business costs. But it is important for any property investor to focus on the profits of capital gains earned and not on business costs. To achieve that, investors have to make sure that they invest in properties located in good areas that have the potential for capital growth and increased demand.

Sometimes it is possible to get a mortgage without early payment penalties offered by lenders, but such mortgages are not always available. As part of the early discussion with the mortgage advisors about refinancing, it is always worth asking them if such an option is available. Bridging mortgages which are often expensive in comparison to "normal" mortgages could be an option as well. Bridging mortgages are useful for short-term lending, for example, to buy derelict properties from auctions to renovate, add value, and then rent or sell. Bridging mortgages are also useful for properties with legal or technical problems; these are often sold BMV (below market value) and so it can be difficult to get "normal" mortgages for such properties. Unlike active investors who are willing to invest in properties with problems and invest during uncertain market conditions, banks are often reluctant to offer funds regardless of how small the problems are. This makes bridging mortgages an accessible option to investors to fund their investment projects.

Bridging mortgages are useful for short-term lending, for example, to buy derelict properties from auctions to renovate, add value, and then rent or sell.

During the COVID-19 pandemic period in 2020, income-producing properties continued to work for their owners with limited problems. However, banks were reluctant to approve mortgages or refinance applications due to the challenging situation and uncertainty. They applied stringent lending requirements which had an impact on property business during the pandemic period. However, the business bounce back loans introduced by the UK government made the refinance delays less painful for many real estate investment companies.

Summary

This chapter introduced the subject of real estate investment which entails putting capital into an income-producing asset using one or more classes such as rental income, capital gains, or dividends from REIT(s) shares. However, investors need to follow a particular business philosophy to lead to a successful investment. Some of the UK government's ways of dealing with the real estate industry such as rules and regulation development and their implications were discussed. The main types of residential and commercial properties, as well as useful information about property prices, were presented. Also, this chapter discussed some of the skills and knowledge required by investors to establish a successful real investment such as selecting the right properties located in an attractive place. Therefore, the next chapter will discuss the importance of choosing the right property location in real estate investment. Because property location depends on different factors such as proximity to a CBD, local services and amenities, investors need to consider such issues when they select their best deals. Investing in an income-producing property located in the right area can generate substantial revenue.

Real Estate Location and Selection

6

In real estate investment, property location can determine whether the price is above or below the average. Property location relates to various factors such as distance to a CBD (central business district), and proximity to local services, amenities and attractions. Property investors should be aware of the importance of investment location and how they select their best deals based not only on property location but also the property situation and the seller's circumstances. Investing in residential or commercial properties located in good areas can generate substantial rental income, good profits, and/or promising capital gains. Property location matters and selection criteria are presented in this chapter.

Property Location

Cities develop because of various economic factors which drive major business decision making by investors, commercial businesses, and local governments. Property location plays a major role in its price; often the closer it is to a CBD (central business district) i.e. a city centre, the higher the price. There are cases where edge cities have their own subcentres which attract firms and businesses as well and can drive prices up. An edge city is a mixed-use suburban area outside a CBD having a concentration of residential and business buildings. According to the land rent theory, rent price depends on land location and its usage. Land rent theory states that as we move closer to CBDs we are more likely to pay more for real estate due to higher demand. CBDs often see population growth due to various economic factors such as land accessibility, good transport services, high employment rates, and affordable housing at the outskirts of the CBD.

> Property location plays a major role in its price; often the closer it is to a CBD (central business district) i.e. a city centre, the higher the price.

Figure 6.1 shows a satellite image of Europe and North Africa at night. It's apparent that the strong light spots highlight the major cities alongside their CBDs. Considering the level of services provided by CBDs and their characteristics, city centres appear to be more attractive to firms and retailers than to families and manufacturers who are often pushed outside. Figure 6.2 shows the land rent curves which represent the land usage pattern in a typical city. As CBDs grow, more outskirt locations are being used, attracting increased development of high-rise buildings in CBDs, thus driving rent prices up.

In many CBDs, manufacturing sites have been replaced with commercial units attracting other services, businesses, and retail parks. Successful cities are reinventing themselves as service-driven economies with quality office space and high-rise buildings. They tend to grow to create distinctive areas for businesses and then become interesting places for investment. Central locations attract higher real estate prices for the following reasons:

- Central locations act as a hub for local, national and international firms and provide quality hospitality services and transportation links
- Various economic factors such as high employability rates and know-how centres tend to attract higher property prices
- They provide the benefits of agglomeration economies and recruitment agencies as well as access to skilled workers and heavily populated areas
- Despite the higher costs, central locations provide access to quality office space, enhanced service delivery, and high-rise buildings
- They attract individuals and couples because of job opportunities, access to information and quality services as well as training and education opportunities

Figure 6.1 Satellite image of Earth's city lights. Source: NASA/iStock

Firms and commercial businesses prefer to locate in central areas because of the attractions that they provide despite the higher land prices. Retail businesses are willing to pay higher property rental prices at a central location to benefit from agglomeration economies and access to services necessary to their business such as quality delivery services. However, due to higher property prices in the city centre, people prefer to live at the outskirts where the property prices are less expensive. People are willing to pay for expensive transportation to travel to the city centre in return for affordable housing prices.

By contrast, manufacturers are not attracted to city centres because of higher land prices, high traffic, and limited access to motorways. They would rather locate outside cities and closer to accessible transportation links and cargo railway networks to reduce delivery costs. Manufacturers often need access to large warehouses to store their products and machinery. Therefore, developing such large warehouses requires a larger area of land which would only be affordable outside city centres.

> Firms and commercial businesses prefer to locate in central areas because of the attractions that they provide despite the higher land prices.

> People are willing to pay for expensive transportation to travel to the city centre in return for affordable housing prices.

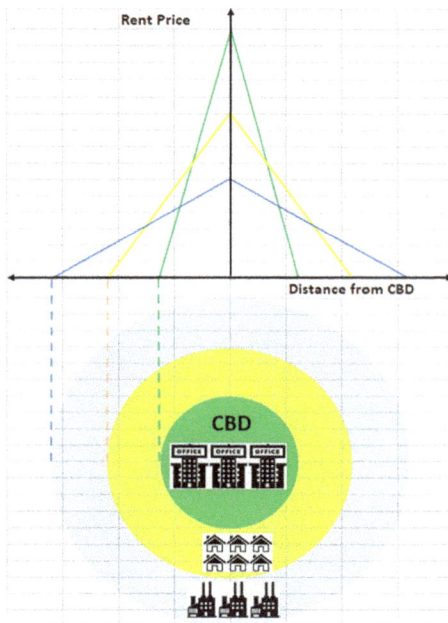

Figure 6.2 Land rent curves

Property Location and Rental Market

Property rental rates are often determined by their proximity to local services, amenities, and attractions. Another economic factor that is used to determine the rent charged to tenants is demand. Properties close to central places often attract potential tenants. Therefore, an investor would use a property's location and nearby services and attractions to their advantage and market it accordingly. The right location can be used as justification to charge higher rates than a competitor, despite the similarity of properties in terms of their size, design, and structure. The pricing structure for rents is dependent not only on location but also on supply and demand as well as market conditions.

> The right location can be used as justification to charge higher rates than a competitor, despite the similarity of properties in terms of their size, design, and structure.

The occupancy levels in the area and the pricing behaviour of competitors will also play a role in the investor's rental rate decisions. It is important for investors to monitor and review local rental rates regularly and price theirs accordingly. This is necessary to ensure business sustainability and avoid both under- and overcharging their tenants. The principles of property business teach us that the more individuals contact the investor about renting a property, the higher the rates an investor can charge i.e. the greater the demand, the higher the rental rates. There can be situations when investors need to drop their rents to compete with other rental rates in their local area, but they must never lose sight of profit margins. However, investors have to be practical and flexible with their rates to attract tenants; they also need to be aware of what their minimum rental rates should be. This will ensure that the property is re-mortgageable when prices increase in the near future.

Investors need to calculate monthly costs and overheads associated with their property and then add planned net cashflow to determine their charged rate. This is to ensure that their property is producing the right profit and able to pay for its management, monthly mortgage commitment, and maintenance costs. Failure to perform this step could result in barely producing enough rent to cover overheads despite achieving good occupancy rates. Finding the best locations therefore requires proper research and information gathering processes. Before making any decisions, investors should collect information about the following:

- Local government developments
- Transport infrastructure improvements
- Universities and schools
- Train stations
- Hospitals
- Business parks
- Local parks
- Distance to the city centre
- Local amenities

Property investors should be aware of the importance of investment locations and how they appeal to certain communities. The demographic makeup of the population plays a role in specifying the market rent, types of properties needed, and the level of demand. Certain communities tend to have specific property design requirements and prefer to cluster near locations that provide services they use often. For example, families with young children like to have easy access to facilities like swimming pools, playgrounds, etc. Understanding the local communities' requirements can also help us understand why certain businesses and facilities enter and set up in those areas. This is important when considering investment locations. The result of such investment decisions is delivering the required type of properties that appeal to certain customers and satisfy their needs. This process of market analysis tends to help with developing an investment strategy that maximises yields and revenues. Therefore, yield does vary by location which significantly affects profitability. An investor needs to acquire the following necessary skills and knowledge:

> Certain communities tend to have specific property design requirements and prefer to cluster near locations that provide services they use often.

1. Study and analyse the property economics and local marketplace
2. Know the competition and how the market operates
3. Understand the levels of supply and demand
4. Select the right location and business area
5. Learn to deal with stakeholders such as banks, mortgage advisors, solicitors, estate agents, local authorities, planners, builders etc.
6. Learn to deal with clients and customers
7. Learn to deal with legal matters such as contracts and formal tenancy agreements
8. Be aware of what constitutes a substantial renovation, maintenance works, associated costs etc.

Also, professional investors committed to building and growing their property portfolio should consider the following:

- Creating a healthy working environment: build trust and treat employees fairly, have good communication in the workplace as well as support for workers in terms of wages, training opportunities, holiday entitlement etc.
- Maintaining a positive outcome: make sure that their income-producing portfolio is expanding and helping them achieve their goals
- Selecting the right business strategy: to be focused on the business, applying the business model that works for them and making the necessary decisions
- Using the correct tools and systems: making use of the right tools, online resources, and systems to support the business such as Xero accounting software, OpenRent online rental property marketing, etc.
- Protecting their assets: using the necessary property insurance, gas safety and electric certification, EPC (Energy Performance Certificate), etc.
- Getting the right advice from professionals: from property solicitors, property accountants, mortgage advisors, surveyors, estate agents, etc. All these professionals represent the investor's power team

Like a shock to the global economy, the COVID-19 crisis has caused turmoil in the financial market and real estate industry. This has been due to the economic disruptions, supply chain interruptions, lockdown measures and rise of unemployment, despite the government's short-term financial support to businesses and individuals. It is going to be a tenant's market in CBD areas because of the expected lower occupancy rates, as many firms have started laying off employees and promoting working from home. They are also relying on the web and technology to carry out their business operations and arrange meetings using tools such as Zoom, Google Meet etc.

Investors might find themselves offering discounts to retain their tenants due to lower demand on office space and residential properties in CBDs. However, active investors can oversee market fluctuations, adapt to changes, and look for opportunities, by making use of their research skills to find bargains and their negotiation skills to buy BMV (below market value) properties, not necessarily in CBDs and central locations but also in areas where demand is still high or above average. One option is to invest in certain types of properties and apply for a change of use to meet the demand for emerging needs for both the government in terms of social distancing and tenants' demands for properties with larger rooms and gardens.

It is not too late for investors who are willing to take risks to find good deals, add value, and then rent or sell in the future when demand picks up. Although it is hard to predict the length of such a crisis and its effects on demand, active investors will continue monitoring and examining the current situation to figure out how to deal with the unprecedented levels of uncertainty and market changes, and fulfil the demand for the real estate industry. Overall, investors who are careful with their investments in terms of the selection of property location, type of tenants, high yielding properties and setting long-term lease agreements will be able to survive and continue with their business with minimum risk and minimum loss.

It is not too late for investors who are willing to take risks to find good deals, add value, and then rent or sell in the future when demand picks up.

Property Selection

The key to successful property investment is finding deals, understanding the market, and proper information gathering. There are different places where investors can identify not only property location and the current market value of their potential investment but also find good deals. Having a system for information gathering such as automated alerts about new properties on the market is always helpful. Using the right resources, investors should also be able to identify the supply and demand and the average market rents in the area they are interested in. Property websites such as Rightmove and/or Zoopla can allow them to access not only current properties on offer but also their historical data in terms of previous sale prices and sale dates. Be aware that certain postcode areas sell well and others don't. Different areas might require different strategies and there is a difference between a property advertised sale price and its value. In chapter 4 we looked at various resources which provide useful information for property investors about the current market in general and property prices in particular.

The best deals also come from distressed properties and/or motivated sellers where investors can aim for a BMV (below market value) deal and add value to the property. Distressed properties do require quick flipping and marketing before selling or renting. Investors have to make sure they have at least two exit strategy options available i.e. either to sell or rent. It is always useful to work with a good mortgage broker and to make sure that he/she is paid well. A motivated seller is a person who might be dealing with any of the following cases:

- Retirement
- Divorce
- Equity release
- Repossession
- Family expansion
- Chain breaking
- Legal issues
- Refurbishment works
- Financial matters
- Inherited property

Active investors use SWOT (Strengths, Weaknesses, Opportunities and Threats) analysis to assess the current position of the property before they decide whether or not to purchase it. Developing a SWOT analysis table is useful for decision making, as shown in figure 6.3. SWOT is a powerful but simple technique that helps find the positives and negatives of a potential property. Here is a list of issues which investors might need to consider before buying a property for investment.

- The value of the property in the future
- Price history of the property and nearby comparables
- Opportunity to enhance and add value to a property. For example, potential refurbishment and/or extra development such as a good size loft and/or garage conversion or large garden/land for a development project
- Opportunity to split deeds (freehold/leasehold)

> Different areas might require different strategies and there is a difference between a property advertised sale price and its value.

STRENGTHS	WEAKNESSES
• Good deal • High demand • Reputable builders • Good yield and ROI • Good location	• Secure deposit • Mortgage cost • Refurbs cost
OPPORTUNITIES	THREATS
• Extension of land • Garage conversion • Loft conversion • Title splitting	• Planning permission challenge • Interest rate rises • Tax changes

Figure 6.3 SWOT analysis for a potential property

Investors can advertise a newly purchased property even before exchanging contracts or completion. There are various ways that investors can check the demand for their properties in an area. To test the market, investors can find comparables i.e. similar properties for sale/rent using property marketing websites. They can then advertise their selected property for rent to check demand using online marketing and social media such as Facebook community groups or websites such as openrent.co.uk or rightmove.co.uk.

Summary

Property location is an important aspect of real estate investment. In this chapter, various factors which can influence property prices such as property proximity to a CBD, local services, local amenities and attractions have been introduced. The importance of property locations lies in the fact that properties located in a good area can produce substantial revenues and high rental profits. Selecting the right residential and commercial real estate in a good location and with the potential to add value should make a useful investment. Investors should not only be aware of how to select the right property location and how it can impact prices but also be aware of how to diversify their investment and assets. The next chapter discusses the importance of having a diverse investment portfolio and how investors can reassess their portfolios. Asset diversification should help investors to invest in multiple asset classes to improve revenues and establish resilient investment with minimum risk. The benefits of portfolio diversification and the main asset classes such as income-producing properties, properties for capital gains, and/or REITs (Real Estate Investment Trusts) will be discussed. Real estate business with a mixture of investment strategies and an ability to respond to hard market conditions will also be presented.

Overview of Investment Diversification

7

In the real estate business, it is important to consider having a diverse investment portfolio. Investors should reassess their diversified portfolio regularly and real estate business in general. Asset diversification is about investing in more than one asset class to improve earnings and minimise risk i.e. not putting all your eggs in one basket. In this chapter the issue of portfolio diversification is introduced: its benefits, and the three main asset classes in real estate. A diversified real estate investment is a portfolio of different types of assets that has a mixture of strategies such as income-producing properties, properties for capital gain, and/or REITs (Real Estate Investment Trusts) shares. Investors with a diversified portfolio can aim for better business resilience because real estate asset classes respond differently to the same market conditions and during difficult economic times.

Portfolio Diversification

Real estate investors need to monitor their market and plan to develop their strategies for growth and expansion. Business diversification is about entering a new market and/or providing a new service as a result of a new strategy. Figure 7.1 shows a modified version of the Ansoff Matrix which indicates the four strategies that can be used by real estate investors to grow their investment as part of their business strategy and risk analysis. They are:

> Business diversification is about entering a new market and/or providing a new service as a result of a new strategy.

- **Market Penetration:** This strategy focuses on expanding the current portfolio e.g. increasing the number of existing income-producing properties in an existing rental market.

- **Service Development:** This strategy focuses on introducing new housing services such as HMOs (Housing of Multiple Occupancy) or SAs (Serviced Apartments) to an existing market.

- **Market Development:** This strategy focuses on entering a new market e.g. starting a real estate business in a different city or country using existing housing service(s).

• **Diversification:** Focuses on entering a new market with the introduction of new housing service(s) e.g. investing in a new asset class in a different market or country.

No doubt there are benefits of real estate investment and asset diversification. Diversification can bring new opportunities such as entering new markets, delivering new services, accessing funds, interacting with new clients, dealing with new tools and technologies, etc. Real estate is one of the most diversified businesses and highly profitable income-generating assets.

		SERVICES	
		EXISTING SERVICE	NEW SERVICES
MARKETS	EXISTING MARKETS	Market Penetration	Service Development
	NEW MARKETS	Market Development	**Diversification**

Figure 7.1 Real estate market expansion grid – Adapted from Ansoff Matrix[17]

Asset allocation is about setting a percentage of each asset class in a portfolio such as BTL (buy-to-let) rental properties, capital gains properties, and REITs shares. The allocation of assets can be set up according to an investor's preference and their investment plans. Figure 7.2 shows the three main real estate asset classes. Investors need to know which type of investment to select to earn a return. Any losses from a poorly performing asset class in their portfolio could be offset by the well-performing assets. However, this requires regular monitoring of the business portfolio and of the performance of the asset classes.

Investors need to know which type of investment to select to earn a return. Any losses from a poorly performing asset class in their portfolio could be offset by the well-performing assets.

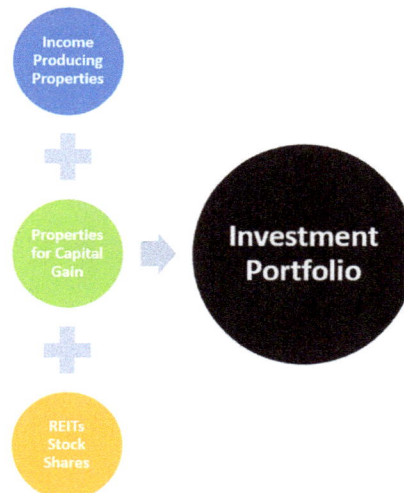

Income Producing Properties

Properties for Capital Gain

Investment Portfolio

REITs Stock Shares

Figure 7.2 Real estate asset classes

Various indicators are used by investors to track the performance of REITs. However, NAV (net asset value) and AFFO (Adjusted Funds from Operations) are the most commonly used indicators to monitor the performance of REITs operations and their financial position. Getting into higher levels of risky real estate investment means investors should expect higher returns and vice versa. However, investors should be wise in their investments and risk-taking and should aim to build an optimal portfolio. An optimal portfolio is an efficient portfolio that provides the highest investment returns and minimum risk. This allows investors to limit the likelihood of incurring income losses because of taking certain financial risk(s). The optimal portfolio uses statistical techniques to quantify and adjust asset diversification according to the investor's plans. This helps investors to achieve their goals of balancing returns and risk.

> Getting into higher levels of risky real estate investment means investors should expect higher returns and vice versa.

Direct and Indirect Investment

There are many different investment types by which investors can invest in real estate. However, the two main types of real estate investments are as follows:

- **Direct:** Investors gain exposure to real estate business with direct purchase of a property. They have full control over the property's purchase and ownership and make decisions about which properties to buy.

- **Indirect:** Investors gain exposure to real estate business without the direct purchase of a property such as via REITs (Real Estate Investment Trusts) stocks. They have less control over the properties purchased and rely on experts to make decisions about which properties to buy.

Direct investment might provide higher returns than indirect investment, but to achieve those higher returns would require more effort and time from the investor. In a direct real estate investment, investors can select the strategy of their investment and choose the properties and location they like. As a property owner, it is the investor's responsibility to check the structural stability of the property they are buying. They have the choice of deciding the capital structure and amount of upfront investment. They are responsible for paying Capital Gains Tax and rental income tax. Also, investors can manage their portfolio themselves, appoint someone, or arrange an agreement with a letting agent to do the work for them. They need to check and negotiate the terms and conditions of the tenancy agreement if necessary.

> Direct investment might provide higher returns than indirect investment, but to achieve those higher returns would require more effort and time from the investor.

In indirect real estate investment, investors cannot choose the properties bought by the REIT or influence the investment strategy. Such matters are left to the experts operating the REIT to decide upon. The investment structure is decided by the experts as well. Investors do not own the properties and cannot manage them or influence their management procedures. Tenancy agreements are arranged by the REIT or their appointed agents directly with their tenants. Investors do not have a say in such crucial decisions and management processes. Indirect investments use market shares that are traded at specific prices for REIT and trades can be executed easily and quickly. Table 7.1 below summarises the difference between direct and indirect real estate investments.

Feature	Direct	Indirect
Property ownership	✓	
Full control	✓	
Property selection	✓	
Expert selection		✓
Faster purchase		✓
Market volatility		✓
Joint venture option	✓	
Traded on a stock exchange		✓
Leverage using building societies and banks	✓	✓

Table 7.1 Comparing direct and indirect real estate investments

Investors might need to think about diversifying their investment portfolio to minimise risk and maximise returns. Investing in one asset class could have an impact on their returns if that asset class unexpectedly fails to perform as well as investors had anticipated. Therefore, spreading the risk over multiple asset classes can provide investors with good asset allocation options, better business resilience, and more confidence. An asset class represents a specific category of investment; therefore, investors need to know how much investment or budget they need to allocate to each category.

REITs (Real Estate Investment Trusts)

As indirect real estate investment, REITs provide property investors with the opportunity to invest in portfolios of income-generating assets. The REIT industry has become popular in many countries and has experienced significant growth around the globe. Many property investors have become aware of REITs investment as a useful option for asset diversification. REITs operate in various property investment activities such as mortgage services and real estate financing, commercial buildings, property development and construction, land and real estate acquisition, etc. Despite the lack of control over which properties are selected, REITs provide a flexible option for investors. REITs experts take care of choosing which properties to invest in. REITs rely on investors to raise additional funds and expand their business; therefore, investors are expected to benefit from REIT returns and to get paid dividends regularly. Investors assess the performance of REITs based on the following factors:

REITs operate in various property investment activities such as mortgage services and real estate financing, commercial buildings, property development and construction, land and real estate acquisition, etc.

- Higher yields
- Larger dividend rates
- Long-term capital appreciation

- Larger portfolio
- Produced profits and balance sheets
- Experience and strong management

Investors in REITs buy shares in a REIT company which means that they own part of the company's properties or portfolio. The share prices tend to fluctuate and investors can buy and sell according to the rules of the business. In the UK, all REITs are publicly listed on the stock exchange market. Each REIT has to meet certain requirements to go through an approval process to be accepted and become listed. The company's share price becomes available for investors and trading. Like direct real estate investment, REITs shares are sensitive to economic changes, interest rate fluctuations, and central banks' monetary policies and regulations.

Unlike other traditional stock markets, REITs are less volatile due to the relative stability of the real estate market. Investing in REITs stock shares can be a good option for investors to not only diversify their investment business but also to improve their investment portfolio and make it more resilient. REITs are set up as companies or trusts and once they become active and start a business, they pay part of their earnings from rental income and capital gains as dividends to their shareholders. The main five types of REITs are:

- **Residential REITs:** invest in apartment blocks and family renting market. They focus on areas where there is a large demand, higher occupancy rate, and good rental income.

- **Office REITs:** specialise in office buildings such as law firms, accountants, banks, etc. and often focus on CBD (central business district) areas due to large demand and higher rental income.

- **Retail REITs:** specialise in shopping centres and retail parks. They generate rental income from their tenants i.e. the retailers. Recently, the retail business has been under pressure due to the shift to online shopping.

- **Mortgage REITs:** invest in mortgages, financing, and secured and unsecured loans. They generate income from interest on those investments. Their stock prices and financing services are influenced by interest rate changes. Historically, mortgage REITs are known for their relatively high dividends.

- **Healthcare REITs:** specialise in hospitals, retirement apartments, nursing homes, and healthcare services. It is a growing business due to increased demand for healthcare buildings and services. However, healthcare REITs are under pressure due to the recent challenges of COVID-19.

When REIT share prices increase, investors should benefit from capital growth and make a profit, but they may lose money if the share price of the REIT falls. Falling share prices of a REIT company can have a negative impact not only on investors but also on the company's reputation and future business. Successful REITs tend to invest in a well-developed, financially robust, and diverse portfolio of real estate in order to mitigate any risks or market volatility. The higher the value of the shares and stocks over time the better the payout of dividends. Many REITs offer their shareholders dividend reinvestment plans in additional shares of the company. Investors can check if such an option is available for them before committing to an investment. REITs with such a feature can accelerate the compounding rate and achieve a higher rate of growth in comparison with those which do not offer reinvestment plans.

Summary

Real estate investment diversification is a useful way for investors to improve their revenues and develop resilient portfolios. Investors should consider reassessing their portfolios regularly and investing in multiple asset classes to seek opportunities and minimise risk. This chapter introduced the principles of investment diversification, the main types of asset classes, and their benefits to investors. As an investment asset class, REIT implies owning REITs shares as a percentage of REITs properties and receiving dividends annually. Using a mixture of investment strategies including sustainability and investing in sustainable REITs can help investors achieve better profits and respond to unpleasant market conditions. Real estate markets, the issue of sustainable real estate and the contribution of real estate to greenhouse emissions which could lead to different environmental problems will be presented in the next chapter. Investing in sustainable real estate should help investors access new opportunities such as financial and social benefits. The next chapter will also discuss how investors' use of government incentives and green policies can help through developing sustainable buildings, reducing greenhouse emissions, and bringing financial and social benefits.

Investment Diversification and Sustainability

8

Investing in a diversified portfolio with a mixture of strategies can help investors to use multiple asset classes in their business. This will improve revenues, develop resilient investment, and minimise risk during adverse market conditions. Investing in REITs shares in the stock market implies owning a percentage of REITs properties and receiving dividends annually. This chapter introduces REITs markets and provides examples of REITs listed companies. Investing in multiple strategies such as sustainable REITs can bring more benefits to investors. Real estate contributes to carbon emissions, and has an impact on climate change. This chapter also discusses how governments are developing policies and using different mechanisms of rating systems to assess the sustainability of properties. One way to reduce energy consumption and greenhouse emissions is to consider investing in sustainable buildings to minimise losses and bring financial and social benefits. The general aspects of real estate sustainability are introduced at the end of this chapter.

REITs Market

REIT investors would expect to receive regular reports about the generated earnings and capital gain portion. REITs are governed by local regulations and legislations of the jurisdiction in which they are set up and must meet their criteria to practise business. There are about 50 REITs listed on the London Stock Exchange which invest in various asset classes such as office, residential, hotel, and retail. Figure 8.1 shows the London Stock Exchange FTSE 350 – Real Estate Investment Trusts REITs Streaming Chart during the period from January 2011 to July 2020. The REIT market has reacted unpredictably like many other stock markets with large drops during the March to June 2020 period due to the COVID-19 pandemic. Figure 8.2 shows the top REITs companies trading on the London Stock Exchange as of 31 January 2020. In the UK, REITs must meet the following main criteria and requirements to carry out business:

> REITs are governed by local regulations and legislations of the jurisdiction in which they are set up and must meet their criteria to practise business.

- Practise trading on an established and recognised stock market exchange. In the USA, REITs are not required to be listed on public stock markets
- Pay at least 90% of rental income to shareholders each year
- 75% of total earnings should be from real estate rental income

- UK resident for tax purposes
- Investors follow tax procedures and regulations
- Solely involved in the property investment business with at least three properties

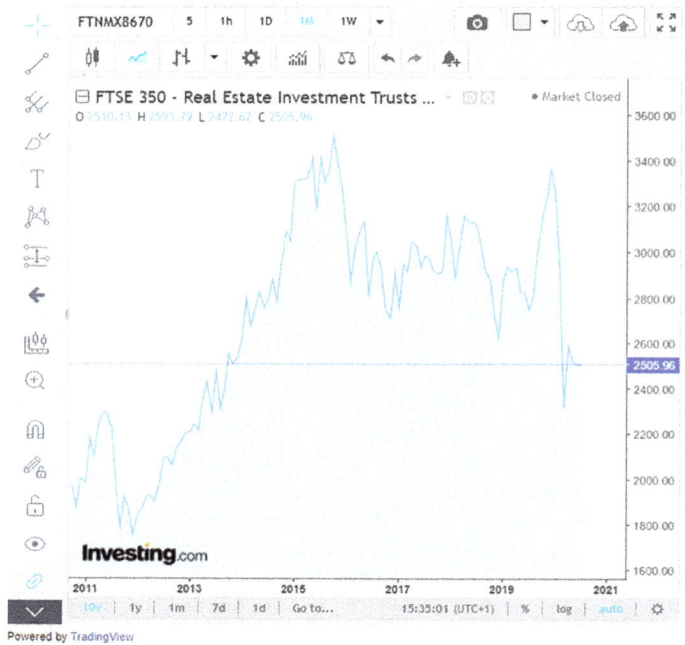

Figure 8.1 FTSE 350 REITs streaming chart (Jan 2011–July 2020) – Source: https://uk.investing.com/indices/ftse-350-reits-chart

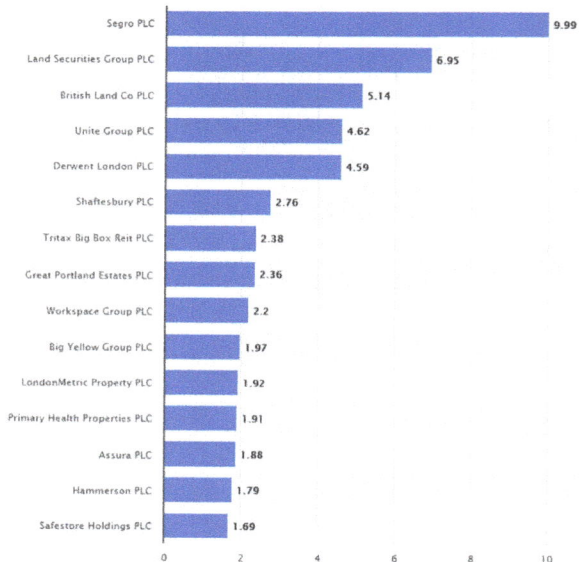

Figure 8.2 REITs Market capitalisation (in billion British pounds) – Source: https://www.statista.com/statistics/325371/uk-lse-reits-ranked/

The Investment Property website https://investmentproperty.co.uk/ provides useful information on the UK REITs market and business. It provides helpful guidance to real estate investors who are seeking investment opportunities in the UK's REITs. Nareit's website https://www.reit.com/ is a useful resource and presents publicly traded real estate companies in the US market to the global investment community. As an investor, I give priority to direct real estate investment, because I like to have full control of my properties, self-manage the business through my property business company anzar.co.uk and to have flexibility in terms of selecting which type of properties to invest in. This does not mean that direct investment is better, but each investor has their preferences and business priorities. REITs provide a useful option for portfolio diversification and there are various REIT platforms that people can use and which offer different levels of returns for potential investments.

REITs investors and stakeholders are increasingly recognising that buildings are large consumers of energy and a major pollution contributor. As a source of pollution, real estate contributes to carbon emissions, produces a large amount of waste, and has an impact on energy consumption and the climate. Investing in multiple strategies such as sustainable REITs is more critical than ever. Sustainable REITs can bring enormous benefits to both property investors and tenants. Investors who are considering sustainable REITs will be better positioned for the risks and opportunities in terms of cost-saving, increased revenues, energy-efficient performance, tenants' wellbeing, and building resilience against climate change.

Sustainable Real Estate

Real estate contributes significantly to greenhouse gas (GHG) emissions which could have an impact on climate change. Governments need to develop the necessary policies and implement the required measures to minimise the impact of carbon emissions and the effects of climate change. Therefore, investing in green buildings and sustainable practices in construction and new developments can bring financial and social benefits and reduce energy consumption and greenhouse gas emissions. Such benefits can bring potential value for property developers, tenants, investors, and society as a whole. The growth in rent for sustainable buildings is expected to become bigger than that from non-sustainable buildings regardless of their locations.

> *"Buildings are a key component in the fabric of cities. And the building and construction sector is one of the most important areas of intervention and provides opportunities to limit environmental impact as well as contribute to the achievement of sustainable development goals [...] Numerous studies have also shown a relationship between buildings and public health. At the same time, the built environment accounts for a large share of energy (estimated to be about 40% of global energy use), energy-related greenhouse gas emissions (estimated to be approximately 30%), waste generation and use of natural resources."*
> The UN Environment Programme (UNEP)[18]

As an investor, I give priority to direct real estate investment, because I like to have full control of my properties, self-manage the business through my property business company anzar.co.uk and to have flexibility in terms of selecting which type of properties to invest in.

The growth in rent for sustainable buildings is expected to become bigger than that from non-sustainable buildings regardless of their locations.

According to the bid rent theory, prices for properties tend to increase as the distance from the CBD decreases due to increased demand. Therefore, sustainable (or green) buildings are expected to achieve a substantial increase in rental income especially if located at a central location within the CBD. Certified green properties are likely to achieve a higher rental income and are expected to grow gradually in the future as well. Unlike green properties, non-sustainable buildings are not expected to achieve a high increase in rent, especially if they are not close to the CBD.

There are different mechanisms of rating systems developed to assess the sustainability of properties and development projects. BREEAM (Building Research Establishment's Environmental Assessment Method) is the UK-based leading sustainability assessment and rating scheme for buildings, construction projects, and the built environment lifecycle. BREEAM operates at a global level and is considered as one of the major tools for sustainability assessment. It uses well-established standards in sustainable methods to attract green property investments and protect natural resources. The World Green Building Council, which is also a recognised global entity, has identified three categories of green buildings benefits[19]:

- **Environmental:** Green buildings can offer benefits to our climate and natural environment by reducing carbon emissions and improving energy and water consumption.

- **Economic:** Financial and economic benefits can be achieved by introducing cost savings on utility bills and improving rates of energy spending and water efficiency.

- **Social:** Green buildings can bring positive impacts on social matters such as brain function, tenants' wellbeing, and sleeping habits.

Sustainability and Government

Some governments tend to encourage the development of sustainable buildings by offering financial incentives, in particular using property tax assessment incentives. The UK government uses various tax regimes to encourage businesses and property investors to invest in environmentally sustainable buildings. The aim is to improve the quality and energy efficiency of buildings by using solar panels to generate electricity, efficient water taps, and heating systems, etc. Environmental taxes encourage landlords and property investors to operate in a more environmentally professional way. Investors and property developers in the UK can expect relief from certain taxes when they invest in sustainable buildings and use energy-efficient technologies in their buildings.

Environmental taxes encourage landlords and property investors to operate in a more environmentally professional way.

As part of the UK's commitment to improving the energy efficiency of UK homes, the government launched the Green Finance Strategy in 2019. The purpose of this strategy is to support the UK financial sector in developing green mortgage products. Green mortgages are useful low-rate loans for financing energy-efficient property projects to reduce emissions from UK homes. The idea behind these discounted mortgage products is to encourage landlords to consider green investment, upgrade the energy efficiency i.e. EPC (Energy Performance Certificate) rating, and ultimately mitigate the impact of climate change. Figure 8.3 shows the EPC register website. The EPC scale starts from A as the highest level to G as the lowest.

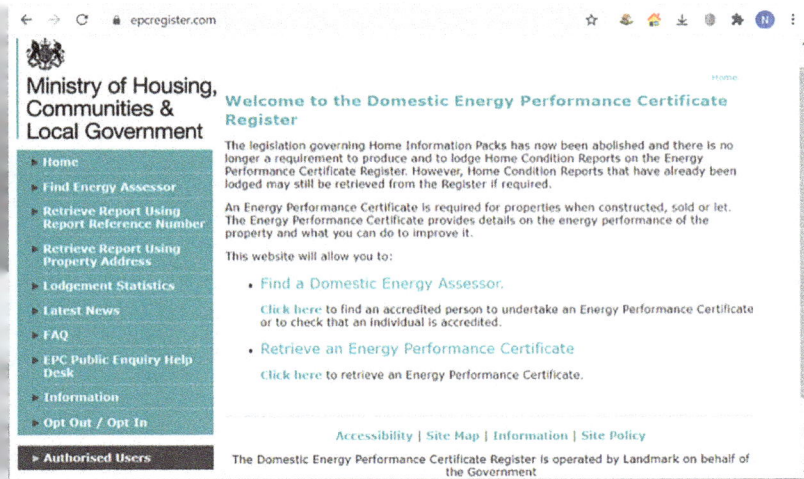

Figure 8.3 The EPC Register website

EPC is a legal requirement that has to be arranged by landlords. Within my development and investment companies, when a property needs refurbishment work, it is necessary to check the property's energy consumption performance (its EPC rating) as part of the property sustainability checks. It is used to check the level of insulation for saving energy. Improving the efficiency of energy consumption through better wall insulation, using LED lights, and/or installing solar panels can help with the EPC rating, making refinancing and remortgage applications stronger and giving one a better chance of obtaining a green mortgage. It is always useful to check the validity of a property's EPC and make sure that it is up to date.

EPCs are available online for most properties in the UK and when issued they become valid for ten years. In my property business, when an EPC is about to expire for a particular property, we call a specialised engineer in to do the required checks. If the EPC is successful, we get the certificate; if not, we ask the same engineer if available to carry out the necessary works and then get the property certified, otherwise we ask another engineer to do the works. Figure 8.4 shows part of an EPC for a particular house. The EPC certificate indicates that the current Energy Efficiency Rating is C which is within an acceptable range. The EPC is an important document that needs to be provided to the tenant as part of the tenancy agreement documents.

In my property business, when an EPC is about to expire for a particular property, we call a specialised engineer in to do the required checks. If the EPC is successful, we get the certificate; if not, we ask the same engineer if available to carry out the necessary works and then get the property certified, otherwise we ask another engineer to do the works.

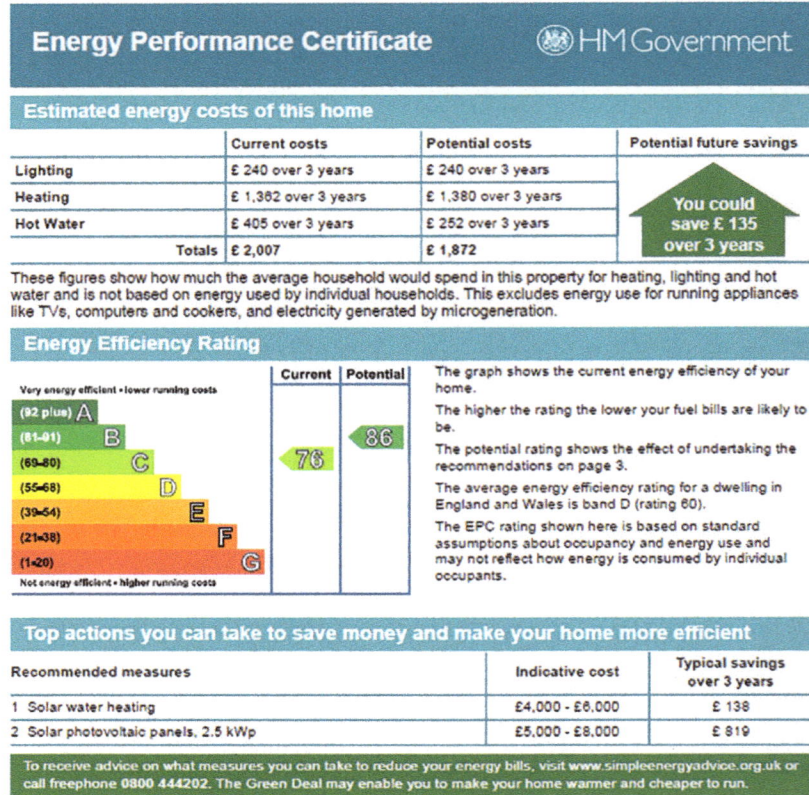

Figure 8.4 Part of an EPC Certificate

In March 2011, the UK government announced the Renewable Heat Incentive (RHI) policy to support renewable heat generation projects to replace fossil fuels and reduce greenhouse gas emissions. The support scheme started in 2014 to encourage the use of renewable heating systems among domestic customers to minimise carbon emissions. The purpose is to encourage landlords, commercial and industrial businesses to consider the installation of renewable heat systems such as solar energy technologies and heat pumps in their buildings. It is a long-term financial incentive scheme to improve the quality of, and the way heat is produced and consumed inside properties.

Investing in sustainable buildings can result in much more rental income than the costs incurred to maintain them due to lower operating and financial costs. Because there is an increasing demand from tenants who prefer to occupy environmentally-friendly properties, sustainable buildings are expected to achieve higher net operating income in the future. Property growth is more likely to occur for green buildings due to lower maintenance costs, higher demand, and greater occupancy. Also, higher sale prices of sustainable buildings can attract higher rents in comparison to non-sustainable buildings. So, investors are expected to achieve capital growth, a higher increase in rental income, and ultimately receive higher returns from green buildings. By making a building more energy-efficient, the investor can expect the property's value to increase which will have a positive impact on the investor's balance sheet and certainly on their business as a whole.

Summary

Real estate investment diversification and sustainability provide investors with new challenges but also new opportunities to build healthy portfolios. Using a mixture of investment strategies can help investors to achieve better profits and respond to different market conditions. Investing in multiple asset classes and sustainable properties as well as seeking opportunities such as green mortgages can bring different benefits to investors and tenants as well as financial and social benefits. Also, investors can make use of the information provided by estate agents to find out the energy efficiency of properties advertised for sale. The next chapter introduces estate agents and the issue of selecting the best deals by investors based on the property situation and the seller's circumstances. Estate agents are a useful source of information about properties for sale and their condition and for granting access to advertised properties. The way investors need to deal with estate agents and negotiate prices with them represents an important part of the purchase process towards buying an investment property. All these issues and how investors need to prepare themselves before approaching estate agents and their solicitors will be discussed in the next chapter as well.

Estate Agents

9

In real estate investment, property investors should be aware of how they select their best deals based not only on location but also on the property situation and seller's circumstances. Estate agents can help investors receive such information about the current status of the property and its vendors. Dealing with estate agents represents a crucial step towards purchasing a property as discussed in the first part of this chapter. Investing in residential or commercial properties requires a lot of organisational and communication skills, knowledge gathering, and access to information.

Estate agents provide a crucial service to property investors in terms of access to information, price negotiation, and access to properties for sale. Investors need to be well prepared with the necessary documents such as bank statements, DIP (decision-in-principle) if they are taking out a mortgage, ID, etc. before initiating negotiations with an estate agent. This chapter ends with a useful discussion about how investors deal with estate agents, price negotiations, and property conveyancing

Dealing with Estate Agents

Estate agents play a major role in the real estate business in general. They provide a crucial service to property investors by providing access to properties for sale. Estate agents support sellers to market and sell their properties. Estate agents are qualified to manage the process of property sale and negotiation. Estate agents always try to match buyers with sellers in terms of needs and motives. Vendors pay estate agents to work on their behalf to sell their properties and make sure that the buyers are committed to the sale. It needs to be borne in mind that the process of buying a house in England and Wales is different to Scotland.

Estate agents act as a bridge between a vendor and a buyer. They liaise with all parties involved in the sales process, not only vendors and buyers but also solicitors, brokers, and surveyors, as shown in figure 9.1. This is to make sure that everyone is playing their part and the purchase process is progressing without any issues. The webpage bestestateagentuide.co.uk can be used to search for the major estate agents in a particular area or city. Estate agents provide property investors with the necessary service, support, and advice throughout the purchase process. All objections and/or concerns from both investors and sellers are dealt with by estate agents.

Investors have to prepare themselves to respond to estate agents' questions when they express an interest in their advertised properties. Estate agents often have a system for handling the purchase process right from the

Estate agents provide property investors with the necessary service, support, and advice throughout the purchase process.

beginning till the end. Buyers are expected to provide preliminary information about their status to the estate agents as follows:

- Finances: Whether the buyer is buying the property with cash or through a mortgage
- Current situation: If the buyer owns a property or is renting, and if the buyer is selling a property to purchase the new one
- Timescale: Whether or not the buyer is willing to complete the purchase soon
- Price range: The expected price offered by the buyer

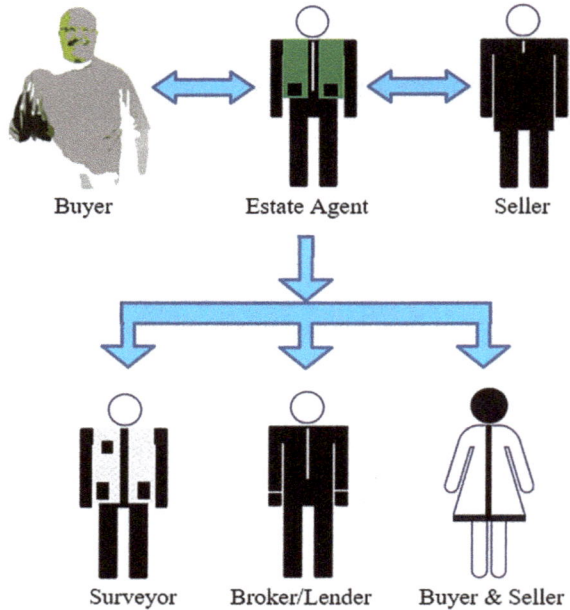

Figure 9.1 The estate's agent relationship with all parties

> Investors have to be prepared to provide all preliminary information and necessary documents because estate agents have to make sure that the buyer/investor is in a position to buy.

Investors have to be prepared to provide all preliminary information and necessary documents because estate agents have to make sure that the buyer/investor is in a position to buy. Recently, estate agents have requested that potential buyers provide more information if they want to view a particular property:

- DIP (decision-in-principle): if they are buying through a mortgage
- Proof of funds: this includes a bank statement to show a deposit or full amount in the case of a cash buyer
- Proof of address: utility bill

However, buyers/investors should expect more documents to be requested. When an offer is accepted, estate agents will request extra details, as follows:

- Proof of identity (ID): Passport or driving licence
- Solicitor's or conveyancer's details
- Mortgage broker's details: if the buyer is buying through a mortgage

Viewing Investment Properties

It is always useful and more helpful for investors to arrange a face-to-face meeting with the estate agent. This will help to build a good relationship and reduce any tensions and competition. It also means an investor becomes more than just a phone number or an email. Estate agents are paid to take care of their clients and make sure that investors are listed in their priority list of buyers' files. Therefore, estate agents will do their best to make sure that the names on their priority list are kept informed when new properties become available for sale. They make sure that their potential investors are invited to view their newly advertised properties if they meet the investors' requirements and conditions. When investors view a property on the market for sale, they should check the condition of the property, as follows:

> Estate agents are paid to take care of their clients and make sure that investors are listed in their priority list of buyers' files.

- Property structure
- Garage(s): for possible future conversion to a room
- Condition of the rooms and garden size
- Indoor damp and mould
- Car park or any parking restrictions
- Windows, doors, kitchen, and bathroom(s)
- The heating system and gas and electric certificates
- Nearby noise from traffic, trains, etc.
- Overlooked by neighbouring buildings

Property investors need to prepare useful questions to ask the estate agents and the vendors about the property. This will help them to find out more about the property and whether there are any issues with the building or its documents. Also, it helps the investor to learn about the vendor and their circumstances. All such information will help the investor to develop a full picture of the building and then to make their final decision whether to buy or not to buy. The following table lists useful questions for an investor to ask an estate agent about the property and vendor.

List of questions an investor should ask the estate agent	
About the property	**About the vendor**
Have any offers been made? If so, how much?	How keen is the vendor to sell?
How long has the property been on the market?	Why are they selling their property?
Leasehold or freehold?	Do the vendors live at the property? If so, how long?
Is there any ground rent and/or service charge?	Are the vendors willing to negotiate on the price?
What is the current rent if the property is rented?	What is the minimum price the vendors will accept?
Is it marked by another agent?	Has the vendor received any offers?
Is it a listed property?	Are the vendors in a chain?
Is the property in a conservation area?	
What will be included in and excluded from the sale?	
Are there any unexpected things to know about this house?	

Table 9.1 Useful questions to ask an estate agent

The Art of Negotiation

Experienced estate agents are well known to be difficult to negotiate with. Therefore, investors need to be well equipped with the necessary knowledge and information before starting any negotiation. It is always useful to negotiate the price before making any offer for a property for sale. A survey carried out by the Department for Business, Energy and Industrial Strategy in 2017 revealed that 51% of successful buyers would negotiate harder on the property price if they bought a property again, as shown in figure 9.2. Listening carefully to what the estate agent's representative is saying is important when you present the starting price offer.

The asking price by the vendor is the price that is highly likely to be accepted. There is no exact figure on how much the starting price should be below the asking price. A range between 10–15% could be a good starting point but it still depends on the asking price and the investor's budget. Investors often keep in mind their maximum price to offer when they start price negotiation. However, the lower the offered price the harder the negotiation with the estate agent is. Neither estate agents nor vendors like receiving awkward offers. Email and social media negotiations are not helpful.

A survey carried out by the Department for Business, Energy and Industrial Strategy in 2017 revealed that 51% of successful buyers would negotiate harder on the property price if they bought a property again.

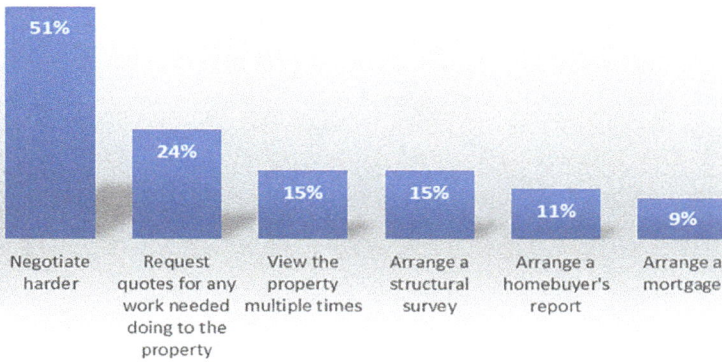

Figure 9.2 What successful buyers would do differently before making an offer – Adapted from *Research on Buying and Selling Homes*, Research paper number BIS/283, October 2017[20]

Estate agents prefer to deal with serious investors who are able and ready to move forward. Letting the estate agent know that a DIP is ready puts an investor in a better position. Estate agents are paid by the seller, so they will try to operate in their own interest and then the seller's interest to get the best deal for them. Once the estate agent receives an investor's offer, they have to pass it to the seller. If the given offer by the investor is accepted then everyone will be happy to move to the next step. The investor can ask the estate agent to

- Not arrange more viewings
- Take the property off the market

This is to avoid "gazumping" i.e. someone else putting in a higher offer than yours.

The same survey carried out by the Department for Business, Energy and Industrial Strategy in 2017 revealed that 88% of the properties were taken off the market after the buyers' offers were accepted by the sellers, as shown in figure 9.3. The remaining 12% of properties were not taken off the market by the estate agents. An accepted offer must be STC (Subject-To-Contract). Estate agents may recommend their solicitors and/or lenders as extra services. It is up to the investor whether or not they use them. However, if the offer is rejected, then the investor has to prepare him/herself for a more rigorous negotiation, as follows:

- Support their negotiation with recently sold comparable properties to justify their offer
- Remind the estate agent of any issues in the property and required refurbishment works
- Be prepared to increase their offer
- Be prepared for uncomfortable negotiations if their offer is rejected again

> Estate agents are paid by the seller, so they will try to operate in their own interest and then the seller's interest to get the best deal for them.

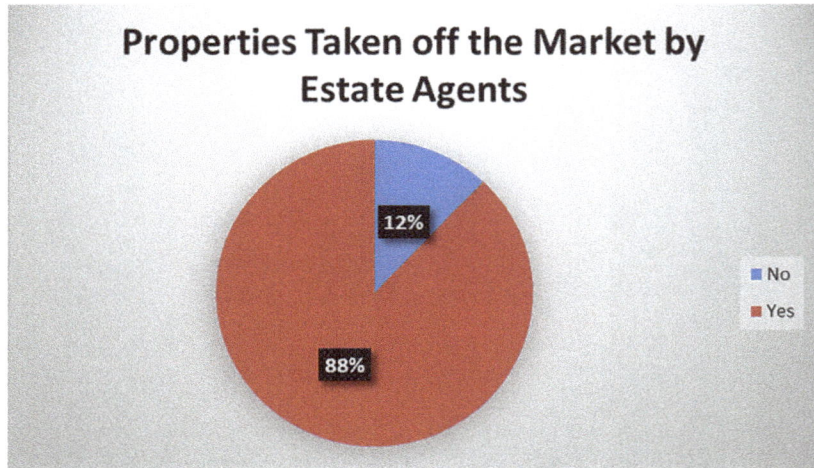

Figure 9.3 Properties taken off the market by estate agents – Adapted from *Research on Buying and Selling Homes*, Research paper number BIS/283, October 2017[21]

The negotiation process may take days or weeks and then lead to nothing. A rejected offer should help an investor to realise the possible value of the property and to reconsider increasing their offer. Estate agents are not expected to disclose other offers by competitors to investors but they would disclose the minimum expected price by the vendor. They often do not know everything about the property, area, or rental market. Unless they have all information and documents about the property, they won't be able to respond to all questions. The majority of estate agents try their best to deliver a quality service and make sure that all parties involved in the purchase process are informed properly, however there are exceptions to every rule. Although rules provide clarity and safety to everyone, we cannot just rely on them all the time to influence people's behaviour and to comply with the rules. Unfortunately, some estate agents try to bend the rules and make an exception but these are the minority. Here is a list of some tricks and tactics used by some estate agents:

- Put their interests first, so they will try to work out how high they can push the price
- Try to make buyers feel as if they are on their side when it comes to making offers
- Encourage a bidding war to get the highest price possible
- Invent non-existent offers to try to convince buyers to raise their bid
- Push buyers to use their own mortgage service and/or solicitors

> The majority of estate agents try their best to deliver a quality service and make sure that all parties involved in the purchase process are informed properly, however there are exceptions to every rule.

Property Conveyancing

Property conveyancing is the process of transferring the legal ownership of a property from one owner to another. The key phases of this process are the exchange of contracts and completion. Property solicitors are specialists in property law and act on behalf of the buyers to take care of the purchase

> Property solicitors are specialists in property law and act on behalf of the buyers to take care of the purchase process and transfer the ownership of a property from the owner to their clients as buyers.

process and transfer the ownership of a property from the owner to their clients as buyers. Part of the solicitor's job is to liaise with all parties involved in the purchase process such as vendor's solicitors, your bank, and the land registry, as shown in figure 9.4. The process of buying a property in England and Wales is different from Scotland. The solicitor will make the conveyancing as hassle-free as possible and carry out the following tasks:

- Deal with all legal matters involved in a property purchase
- Work for the buyer and deal with any of her/his concerns
- Provide the buyer with the necessary service, support, and advice throughout the purchase process
- Carry out the property searches
- Review the draft contract and all relevant documents to check what needs to be investigated
- Exchange contracts with the seller's solicitors and complete the purchase

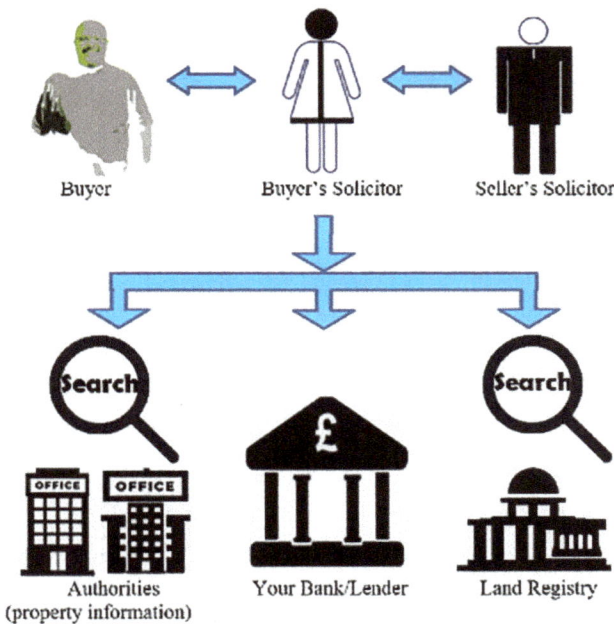

Figure 9.4 Solicitor's engagement with all parties

A property buyer should make sure that he/she has access to a solicitor once their offer is accepted. Do buyers have to use solicitors to purchase a property? No, if they want, the buyers can take care of the purchase process themselves. They have to follow the necessary steps and make sure that they manage the conveyancing process correctly. But if buyers want to use solicitors, they would expect to receive the terms of engagement from them. Property buyers do not expect their solicitors to provide advice on the structure of the property they are buying, its value, the property area, or the rental market. To proceed with the purchase the buyers do so at their own risk. They have to make sure that they are ready to confirm certain information and provide all necessary documents to their solicitors, as follows:

- Sources of funding e.g. savings, joint venture, mortgage, etc.
- ID, proof of address, etc.
- Possession e.g. vacant possession on completion
- Whether they are selling a property to purchase a new one

Solicitors have a system for handling the property file during and after the purchase process. Therefore, some basic knowledge is key when dealing with the solicitors. It is important to listen carefully to what they say but face-to-face meetings are unnecessary. The purchase process may take three to four months and could lead to nothing. Solicitors will carry out pre-contract searches to collect the necessary information about the property from different authorities and the land registry, as shown in figure 9.5. They will check if there are any hidden costs, conditions, financial obligations, and risks. Solicitors will give their clients advice on insurance requested by the bank/mortgage lender if required.

> Solicitors have a system for handling the property file during and after the purchase process. Therefore, some basic knowledge is key when dealing with the solicitors.

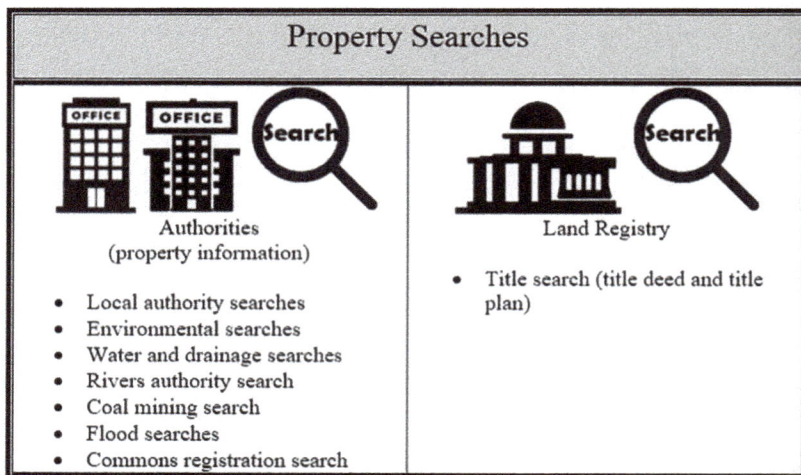

Figure 9.5 Main property searches carried out by solicitors

Property buyers should make sure that they contact their solicitors regularly for updates on the progress of the purchase process. They need to check with their solicitors if there are any issues affecting the legal title in terms of obligations and/or covenants. Any opportunity to strengthen their negotiating position with the sellers would be useful. If the buyers are happy with the information provided by the solicitors, the next step for them is to make their decision: "to buy or not to buy".

The next step is for the solicitors to exchange contracts and obtain a draft contract from the sellers' solicitors. They need to review and check the contract's content in great detail. When both the buyers and sellers as well as their solicitors are satisfied, they can exchange the contracts. Exchange of contracts represents the point at which both solicitors confirm with each other that they hold all the necessary legal documents required for completion, i.e. to complete the transaction. The contract becomes legally binding, i.e. the buyers become contractually committed to the purchase. If the buyers decided to pull out at this stage, then the situation will be treated as a breach of the terms of the legally binding contract, and the buyers must still pay 10% of the agreed price to the sellers. Once the contract has been exchanged, the buyers will not be entitled to any compensation if they decide to pull out.

The buyers can discuss their preferred date of exchange of contracts with their solicitors, preferably the same date as the completion. This is to make sure that the solicitors are able to receive the funds from the mortgage lenders before the exchange of contracts. To achieve that, the solicitors have to contact the lenders to transfer the funds before the exchange of contracts and completion. The buyers should be flexible in terms of the completion date in case there is a chain, i.e. there are multiple related transactions that have to take place at the same time for each property sale and for the purchase to complete. The completion phase represents the final stage of the property purchase. The solicitor will send their clients a completion statement showing them the amount they need to pay which includes:

• Solicitor fees, searches cost, etc.
• Property's full price for cash buyers or deposits if the buyers are using a mortgage
• SDLT if required

The solicitors will confirm the completion date and time with the buyers. The full amount of the deposit and mortgage have to be cleared into the solicitor's bank account before the completion. The solicitors will send the money to the seller's solicitor's bank account and then to the seller's account. Under Anti Money Laundering Legislation, solicitors are prohibited from receiving any cash payments.

After completion, the estate agent will let the buyers know when to come and collect the property's keys. The estate agent needs to receive a confirmation from the sellers' solicitors that the sellers have received the money. The solicitors have to pay the SDLT and send all the legal documents to the land registry to confirm the buyers as the new owners of the property. It shouldn't take long to get the title deeds updated by the land registry and sent back to the buyers' solicitors. The solicitors will send the buyers and their mortgage lenders a copy of the title deeds.

Summary

Estate agents provide a crucial service to property investors through access to information about the status of the property, available deals, the vendor's circumstances, and arranging viewings. This chapter introduced estate agents, their important role in the property purchase process, and in liaising with all entities involved. However, investors need to know how to deal with estate agents in terms of price negotiation, and providing all necessary information and/or documents about their investment plan(s) and financial ability. Investors have to make sure that they are financially ready before starting any negotiations with estate agents, and are aware of the conveyancing process. This involves a lot of preparation and financial planning to avoid using too much of their own capital and having access to funds from third-party entities, which requires some creativity. The next chapter introduces the subject of creative finance which is necessary for structuring a real estate investment project.

Creative finance can help investors prepare themselves when deals become available and can enable them to make purchases using capital from OPM (Other People's Money) legally. This requires certain financial skills and knowledge as well as a clear investment strategy. Various issues related to financial management, using financial techniques such as leveraging, benefiting from the market regardless of the economic conditions, making the right investment decisions, and building wealth using creative finance will be covered in the next chapter. The exploitation of creative finance in real estate investment can help investors to make use of this intelligent model to fund their projects and build their income-generating portfolios. Real-life scenarios supported with practical examples of creative finance for property investment will be presented as well.

Creative Finance 10

Creative finance is an intelligent way of structuring investment deals to build wealth and accumulate valuable possessions legally such as in a portfolio of income-producing properties. Creative financing can be thought of as a financial model for arranging a deal to purchase or finance a property using capital from a third-party institution or OPM (Other People's Money). However, financial management is key to planning and controlling all the creative financial activities and resources of a real estate investment business. The main idea of creative financing is for investors to use financial techniques such as leveraging to expand their portfolios. For example, third-party creative financing can help investors avoid having to use too much of their own capital.

According to the *Cambridge Dictionary*, creative financing is "new or unusual ways of legally getting money to finance something such as a home, project, or business".

Due to accessible funds and current record-low mortgage rates, investors are making proper use of this opportunity to fund their real estate investment projects. The issues of developing income-generating portfolios, building wealth using creative finance, will be introduced in the start of the chapter. This chapter covers the main concepts of property finance including profits produced from rental income and capital growth as well as the costs associated with property business. It highlights the importance of understanding the financial statement including the income statement and balance sheet.

The exploitation of creative finance in the real estate business and in the main phases of building an investment portfolio will be covered. Some examples of creative financing for property deals will also be presented. Proper use of creative finance can help investors benefit from the market regardless of the economic situation and property price fluctuations. Evaluating a deal in terms of produced cash flow, ROI (return on investment), and achieved rental yield will help investors make the right investment decisions.

Income and Creative Finance

Wealth can be thought of as valuable possessions such as a portfolio of income-generating real estate accumulated over time using creative finance and strategy. To achieve that, investors need to monitor the markets closely, update their knowledge regularly, and make sure that they are up to date in terms of skills and news. According to cnbc.com's 2019 report[22], the majority of billionaires worldwide were self-made, but also without too much cash and much funding available to many of them. Individual investors, or groups of

According to cnbc.com's 2019 report[27], the majority of billionaires worldwide were self-made, but also without too much cash and much funding available to many of them.

businesses, set their financial goals, develop and establish their investment plans and projects using creative financial strategies to build up their assets, and to build up wealth, as shown in figure 10.1. In the real estate business, creative finance is used by business-minded individuals as follows:

- Buy what could make an income-generating property using as little of their money as possible to pay for a deposit
- Add value to the property and then
- Refinance the property after it has gone up in value, to release equity, pay off debts, and/or to reinvest.

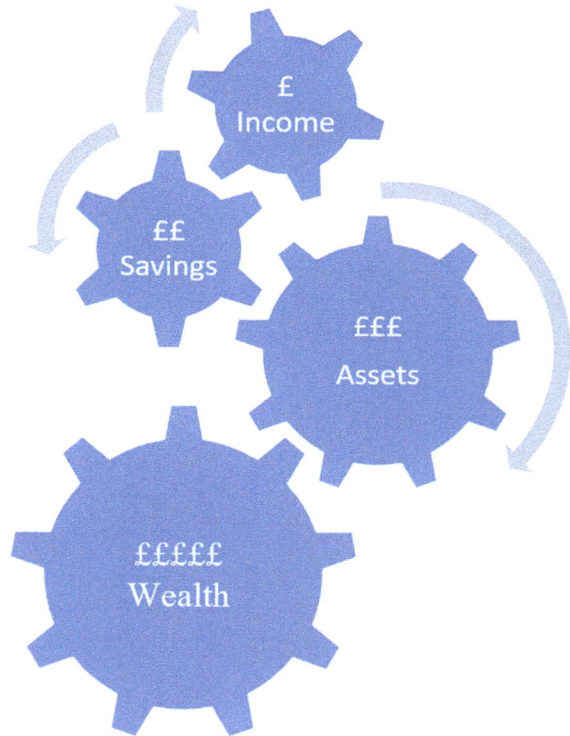

Figure 10.1 Creative finance

For individuals, the two main types of income are as follows:

- **Active income:** earning from delivering a service for an employer or customer i.e. exchanging income for work in which an individual is actively involved e.g. a job.

- **Passive income:** earning without participating or with little effort, where an individual is not actively involved e.g. rental income or as a result of capital growth. Such an income requires some work and extra attention at the beginning to set it up.

Multiple sources of income do help to ensure regular savings. However, whether it is an active or passive income, or a combination of both, keeping expenses lower than income, having a spending plan, managing after-tax income savings regularly, monitoring the budget, and investing carefully are all significant steps to creating wealth. Assets are any accessible cash, from active or passive income, savings, and personal assets such as properties, gold, or items that are convertible to cash. Liabilities represent any debts, regular financial commitments, sometimes unnecessary expenses, and/or fees. They often result from unwise financial decisions which add an extra burden to individuals.

There are two important financial statements for any type of business or investment. These are the income statement, also known as the profit and loss statement, and the balance sheet. The income statement includes the revenues produced from a particular business and expenses incurred to keep the business running. The income statement is produced during a certain period, often the tax year. This statement shows the business's ability to produce profit and/or minimise expenses. The balance sheet includes the assets and liabilities at a specific point in time. It reveals what an individual owns and owes, and their equity.

> The income statement includes the revenues produced from a particular business and expenses incurred to keep the business running.

> The balance sheet includes the assets and liabilities at a specific point in time.

Wealth and Creative Finance

Using the balance sheet, it is possible to determine someone's wealth; that is why lenders are often interested in checking the balance sheet to figure out how much an individual is worth. It can help them assess their financial status and make a decision on whether or not to lend them money. More details about the income statement and balance sheet will be covered in chapter 14, the accounting chapter. Figure 10.2 shows a simplified version of both financial statements, the income statement and the balance sheet. In his book *Rich Dad Poor Dad*, Robert Kiyosaki discussed the importance of understanding the income statement and balance sheet, and the relationship and cash flow between both of them.

Investors focus on growing their assets column using the profits produced from their business revenues and vice versa. This helps them to reinvest and build their wealth. Also, investors manage their liabilities and expenses effectively to reduce any financial risk and continue investing in more assets. However, the majority and the middle class in particular focus on acquiring liabilities instead of assets which implies more expenses. That is why for the majority of people, getting more money or a pay rise often won't solve their problems, and they end up struggling financially. This is because of the following reasons:

- They only rely on their salary
- They spend everything they earn in liabilities
- Their assets are always less than their liabilities, and
- They lack financial knowledge

Income Statement				Balance Sheet	
Company Name				**Company Name**	
Period				Date	
Revenue				**Assets**	
Rental income				Residential properties value	
Dividends				Commercial properties value	
Royalties				REITs stock shares value	
				Gold	
Gross profit				Cash	
Expenses					
Mortgage payments					
Interest				**Total assets**	
Legal and Professional Fees				**Liabilities**	
Insurance				Mortgages	
Marketing				Credit card debts	
Rent				Car finance	
Repairs and Maintenance				Loans	
Supplies					
Internet					
Travel					
Salaries					
Total Expenses				**Total Liabilities**	
Net Income				**Total Equity (Net worth)**	

Figure 10.2 Financial statements

> Active investors tend to reinvest the generated income in order to build more wealth and leverage.

The best way to build wealth is through investment and reinvestment to generate revenues and accumulate income-producing assets. Active investors tend to reinvest the generated income in order to build more wealth and leverage. Leverage is an investment strategy of using different financial mechanisms such as borrowed capital to increase earnings. Real estate appreciates in value, often at a good rate over time. Real estate investment generates income regularly and if this income and savings is reinvested in more properties, rather than spent on unnecessary matters, then the portfolio and wealth will grow in the long term. The earlier they start, the more flexibility there will be to gain the necessary skills and knowledge, the more time to recover from losses, and the more likely they will be to succeed. Wealth represents the total net worth on the balance sheet at any given time, as follows:

Wealth (net worth) = Assets – Liabilities

The wealth or net worth figure is used as an indicator by financial institutions to determine an investor's financial situation at a certain point in time and to decide whether or not to fund their investment. Net worth figures tend to change frequently depending on the level of investment activities, amounts of financial transactions, and projects carried out. Figure 10.3 shows the three main phases of investment for building wealth used by investors, which are:

- Phase one – Save and Build: in the beginning, savings could be used to build the business and to start producing income.
- Phase two – Monitor and Reinvest: monitor the market regularly and reinvest received earnings.
- Phase three – Develop and Leverage: finally develop the business using the appropriate investment strategy to maximise returns and grow wealth.

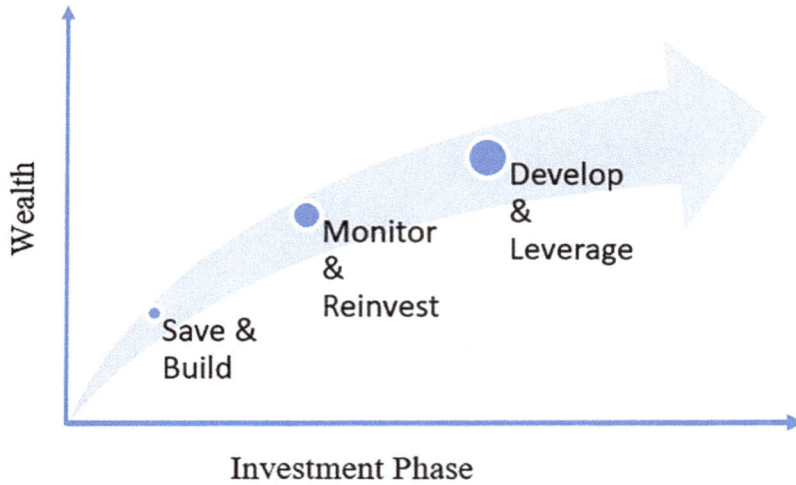

Figure 10.3 Investment phases for building wealth

Investors make sure that their investment business is managed properly, and generating profits with minimal expenditure. Any capital gains produced from their portfolio are reinvested in buying more properties to generate extra rental income and capital gains and so on. This is called compounding. It is challenging for a beginner to set up a real estate business, starting from scratch to develop a successful investment company and build wealth, but that is the case with every start. That is why successful investors tend to invest in themselves as well through learning from experienced investors and attending relevant training about property investment and finance.

As businessman and philanthropist Warren Buffett said, "The best investment you'll ever make is in yourself."

It is challenging for a beginner to set up a real estate business, starting from scratch to develop a successful investment company and build wealth, but that is the case with every start.

Property Finance

Property investment is becoming popular amongst investors worldwide due to low-interest rates offered by banks and good yields achieved. However, there are various expenses associated with the property business such as maintenance, insurance, mortgage costs, management time, etc. which require proper financial operations. Due to limited capital, investors often rely on banks to fund their investment projects. However, investors with sufficient capital still go for the option of getting extra funds from banks. This allows them to invest in more properties and leverage to magnify their returns. Different factors attract investors to the property business. The major three factors are as follows:

1. Return on investment (ROI): Investors use ROI to evaluate the efficiency of their capital investment and measure the amount of return relative to the cost of the investment. It is an indicator used to measure the amount of return on a particular real estate investment.

The basic formula for ROI is:

ROI = (Annual rental cashflow / Initial investment) x 100

Annual rental cashflow = Rental income – Running costs

Initial investment = Cost of investment (e.g. Deposit) + SDLT + Refurbs + Legal fees

SDLT = Stamp Duty Land Tax

Number of years to get back initial investment = 1 / ROI

2. Rental yield: Due to the limited supply of properties, the anticipated demand for renting will be sufficient to expect a good yield and profits. Rental yield is a percentage figure used to calculate the return an investor is likely to achieve on a property through a rental income. The higher the yield the more cashflow investors should expect. We can calculate the rental yield as follows:

Yield = (Annual rental income / Total amount of investment) x 100

Total amount of investment = House price + SDLT + Refurbs cost + Legal fees

3. Capital gain/appreciation: Investors often expect capital apprecia-tion over a particular period from the income-generating property. Any future inflation in the market would contribute to the investor's capital gain.

After calculating the yield, investors may find it useful to determine the maximum offer price for a property which they can provide to the estate agent or the vendor as follows:

Maximum offer = Expected monthly rental income x 12 / Required yield

Sometimes investors get a deal that compounds both rental return and capital growth. The following table shows the main differences between rental yield and capital gain.

Rental Yield	Capital Gain
• Short-term return • Consistent income stream or rental return • Immediate return on an investment	• Long-term growth • Increase in property value • Investors benefit when selling the property or refinancing • Based on historical market data

Table 10.1 Main differences between rental yield and capital gain

Investment and Financing Decisions

To make the right investment decision about a particular property purchase, investors have to ask themselves two questions to evaluate the deal: Does it generate cashflow? And does it have a high yield and ROI? To check whether or not an investment stacks up or not, they have to calculate the net yield, monthly cash flow, and ROI. To achieve that, investors would know the market rent and the mortgage cost (monthly mortgage payment). The cashflow is the profit made from property rent after deducting all expenses, as follows:

Cashflow = Monthly rent – Monthly expenses (Running cost)

Monthly expenses = Mortgage payment + Ground rent + Building insurance + Service charge + Contingency (5%)

The contingency is mainly for other expenses such as management fees, maintenance work, rental voids (lack of rental income) if any, and annual gas safety checks. The following table presents a numerical example of how to calculate the rental yield cashflow and ROI for an income-producing property.

Item	Price (£)
Property price	150,000
Mortgage 80%	120,000
Deposit 20%	30,000
Buy-to-let Stamp Duty (SDLT) 3%, 5%	125,000 x 3% + 25,000 x 5% = 5,000
Refurbs + legal fees	10,000
Value of the property once done	165,000
Rent	900 per month
Yield	**(900 x 12) / 165,000 = 6.5%**
Bank interest rate 3.5%	350
Insurance (monthly)	20
Ground rent (leasehold) and service charge if applicable	0
Contingency 5% per annum	(900 x 12 x 5%) / 12 = 45
Cashflow	**900 − (350 + 20 + 45) = 485**
ROI	**((485 x 12)/45k) x 100 = 13%**
Number of years to get back initial investment	1/13% = 7.7 years

Table 10.2 How to calculate rental yield cashflow and ROI

Selection of an Investment

Property investors often base the success of their investment on the amount of achieved rental yield. High rental yield is an indication of a large demand for rental properties from those who are unable to purchase their own property and fuels rental market and demand. In terms of property prices, renters will expect to pay more when property prices increase. However, homeowners would benefit from the capital gains when they sell their property but investors will have to pay CGT (Capital Gains Tax) for their income-generating properties if they decide to sell.

Property investors can benefit from increased prices as well, not only by selling but also through remortgaging and borrowing more. When property prices increase, active investors will try to expand their portfolios by remortgaging some of their existing properties which have benefited from the increased prices. This enables them to raise funds and make use of these funds to purchase or build more income-producing properties. Figure 10.4 is a flowchart that shows the main steps for selecting an investment property.

Providing more properties will have a positive impact on the supply of residential properties and the rental market. However, due to limited capital, investors often rely on lenders such as banks, non-high street banks,

When property prices increase, active investors will try to expand their portfolios by remortgaging some of their existing properties which have benefited from the increased prices.

crowdfunding, and other investors to expand their portfolios and fund their investment projects. Those with sufficient capital still have the option of using lenders' funds to buy properties and leverage, in order to improve their portfolios and to magnify their returns.

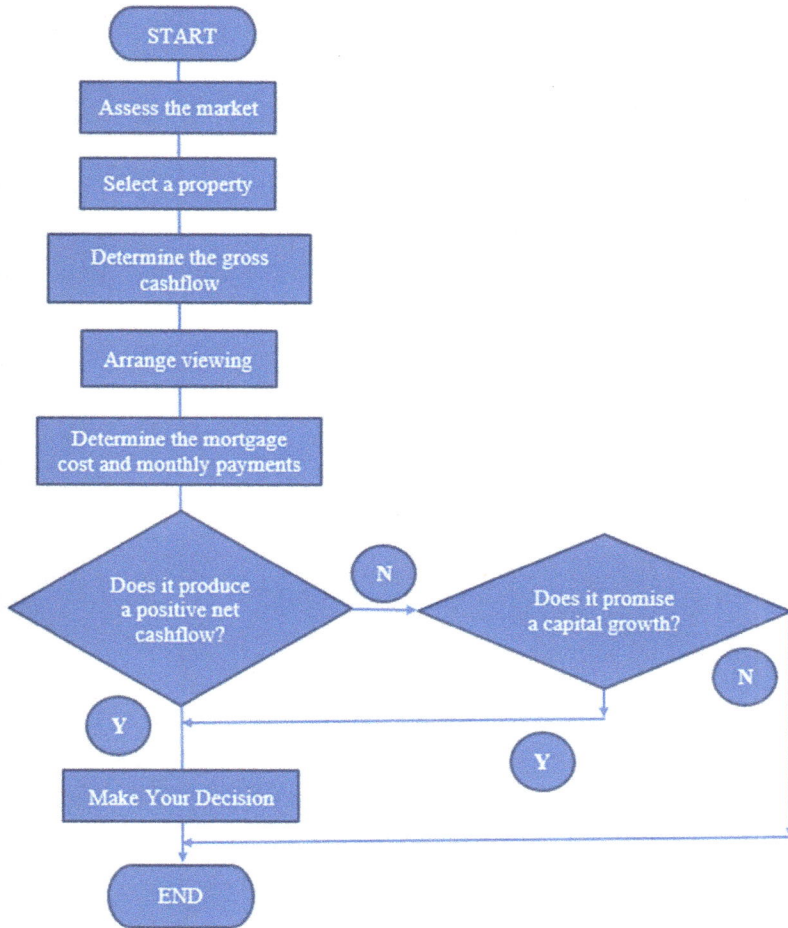

Figure 10.4 A flowchart for selection of an investment property

Summary

Creative finance introduces an intelligent solution for investors to structure their investment deals and build their portfolios. It is a useful way to help investors arrange a deal and finance a real estate purchase using capital from a third-party institution or OPM (Other People's Money) legally. This chapter covered various issues related to this topic including financial techniques and management as a key tool for planning and controlling investment projects. Applying creative finance such as leveraging using available financial products to real-life investment deals can help investors to use the minimum of their own capital. Useful examples supported with real-life scenarios and cashflow and ROI calculations have been presented in this chapter. Investors should be able to exploit creative finance and benefit from the real estate market regardless of economic conditions and price fluctuations.

Creative finance provides an opportunity to resolve the issue of limited access to capital and makes leveraging possible. To achieve this investors should make sure that their income statement and balance sheet are ready for lenders, and have access to funds from high-street or non-high-street banks. The next chapter introduces real estate financing to support investors and fund their deals; however, this requires some preparation from the investor's side such as identifying BMV (below market value) properties if possible, and making sure that deposits are ready in their bank accounts. Banks provide funds in the form of mortgage products with different options of interest rates depending on the length of the term. The process of applying for a mortgage/remortgage, how to receive a mortgage/remortgage offer, and how to determine its interest rate and LTV (loan-to-value) will be discussed in the next chapter. Various topics about how investors can raise funds using creative finance and remortgaging using real-life scenarios of leveraging will be presented as well.

Real Estate Financing

11

Real estate investors should always be prepared to pay a deposit when they purchase a property. However, investors need to identify and get deals preferably BMV (below market value). Banks are the main source of capital for providing different mortgage products and funding investment projects. In this chapter, the process of getting a mortgage and how to determine its LTV (loan-to-value) is introduced. This chapter discusses how investors can raise funds and expand their portfolios using creative financial methods such as remortgaging when property prices increase. Because of the importance of investors using creative finance to raise funds, practical examples and real-life scenarios of remortgaging will be presented.

Mortgage Deposit and LTV

Most banks require investors to pay a deposit of 20–25% of the total purchase price of the property, and they agree to pay the remaining balance of 75–80%. However, investors need to put in an effort to get BMV (below market value) deals for distressed properties or from auctions. This has to happen before agreeing on a price with the vendor(s) or the estate agent. This is to give themselves a chance to sell the purchased property for a profit which can then be used to reinvest in the next property deals and so on. This can be achieved by adding value to the property through quality refurbishment works, adding an extension, or loft conversion. So investors need to be aware of the difference between the property asking price that is the seller's asking price, and the property value which is what the surveyors think.

For an investor to get a mortgage accepted, banks require them to pay a deposit depending on the offered loan-to-value (LTV) i.e. the percentage of the property price offered as a loan to the investor by the bank. Therefore, investors have to understand the mortgage process, the difference between LTV (loan-to-value) and equity, and the difference between buy-to-let and buy-to-sell mortgages. Figure 11.1 shows how a mortgage started with a balance of 75%; as the investor pays the mortgage the LTV decreases, and their equity increases. Notice that by the end of the mortgage period the investor will own the property 100%.

The property market plays a role in determining the value of any property. The property value might fall due to a market downturn to a lower value than the mortgage amount owed to the bank and then the property is said to be in negative equity. Like any market, the real estate business has its ups and downs, and therefore risk management, market analysis, and economics as well as financial intelligence are all important aspects. Also,

The property value might fall due to a market downturn to a lower value than the mortgage amount owed to the bank and then the property is said to be in negative equity.

knowing how to assess the market, identify the right deal, and when to buy, hold, refinance, sell, or exit are important keys to a successful investment.

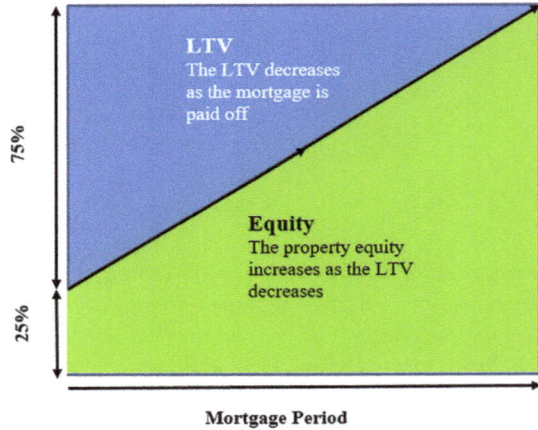

Figure 11.1 LTV and equity

In the property business, investors borrow money from banks to fund their investment projects. Investors need to pay interest which is a percentage of the amount of money they borrowed for their investment. The type of mortgage and interest rates offered will depend on the market conditions and the bank's risk appetite. Banks are willing to finance a variety of real estate assets such as buy-to-let, development, commercial products, etc. They are the main source of capital and mortgage products for property investors. Recently, banks started to offer most of their services online and use mobile banking to support their customers. High-Net-Worth (HNW) customers who have large portfolios and financial assets are well looked after by banks. HNW customers are offered boutique financial services such as wealth planning, family services, and investment advisory services that are not available to average customers. Being a HNW customer has its advantages; they are also allocated financial advisors by the banks.

Banks are willing to finance a variety of real estate assets such as buy-to-let, development, commercial products, etc. They are the main source of capital and mortgage products for property investors.

Funding Investment Projects

There are various options and mortgage products available to investors to fund their investment projects. However, raising the necessary funds for an investment project requires the investor to meet certain conditions and possess marketing skills. A mortgage is a long-term loan taken out by an investor to purchase real estate such as a residential property, land, or commercial unit. The mortgage covers a percentage of the property value known as LTV (loan-to-value) and is secured against the property purchased until it is fully repaid by the end of the term. An investor is expected to put down a deposit as a percentage of the property value and as part of the mortgage agreement.

A mortgage is a long-term loan taken out by an investor to purchase real estate such as a residential property, land, or commercial unit.

The common characteristic of all mortgages is that they will eventually have to be repaid by the investor with interest and/or mortgage charges. If the investor cannot keep up their regular repayments or fails to abide by the agreed terms and conditions, the bank can repossess the property.

Banks can take back the property and sell it to get their capital back. Any remaining money will be paid back to the landlord. The main sources of funding for real estate investment projects are as follows:

- Savings
- Joint venture
- High street banks
- Non-high street banks
- Non-bank financial institutions

In terms of mortgage provision, there are different types of mortgages with different rules and regulations that govern the financial services sector. The two common mortgage types are repayment mortgage and interest-only mortgage. In the repayment mortgage, the property buyer has to pay back the interest and the loan on a monthly basis. The buyer owns the property 100% once they have repaid the interest and loan amount. When using an interest-only mortgage, the buyer repays only the interest on the borrowed loan on a monthly basis. The buyer must repay the borrowed loan amount at the end of the mortgage period. The three common types of mortgages are:

> The two common mortgage types are repayment mortgage and interest-only mortgage. In the repayment mortgage, the property buyer has to pay back the interest and the loan on a monthly basis.

- Fixed-rate mortgage: The interest an individual is charged stays the same for the whole period of the mortgage term regardless of the base rate of the central bank.
- Standard Variable Rate (SVR) mortgage: The interest an individual is charged can change regardless of the base rate of the central bank.
- Tracker mortgage: The interest an individual is charged tracks the base rate of the central bank.

Figure 11.2 summarises the difference between all three mortgage rates.

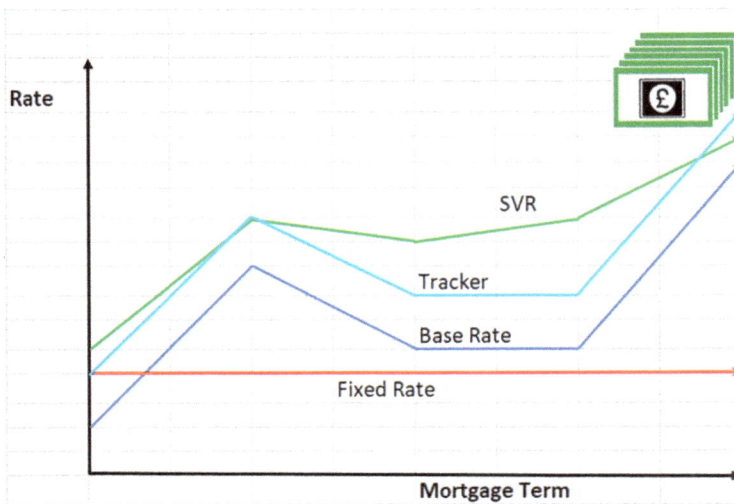

Figure 11.2 Fixed-rate, SVR, and tracker mortgages

Asking a mortgage advisor to get a "no redemption fees/penalties" mortgage product is helpful in case the investor is planning to remortgage their property and raise funds for their next project. Figure 11.3 shows the monthly changes of secured gross funding by UK financial institutions for house purchase and remortgage to individuals during Feb 2013–Feb 2020. Lenders often expect investors to reinvest the raised funds by buying more income-producing properties. This should help the investors to grow their property portfolio and investment. The next time the investor remortgages both their old and recently bought properties that were added to their portfolio, they should use the raised funds to reinvest and buy more income-producing properties, and so on.

Reinvestment helps investors to grow their business, produce better and bigger returns, and has what is known as the snowball effect. As we all know, a snowball gets bigger and bigger when it is rolled down a hill until it becomes a giant ball. Figure 11.4 shows the annual growth of lending to real estate and construction businesses. It highlights the monthly changes of funding to two major non-financial sectors, the construction and real estate sectors. The amounts that are presented in figure 11.4 include both loans and securities.

> Reinvestment helps investors to grow their business, produce better and bigger returns, and has what is known as the snowball effect.

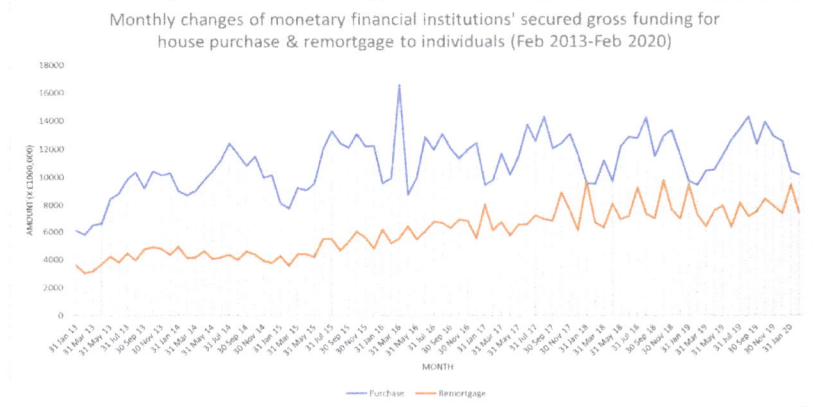

Figure 11.3 Monthly changes in funding for house purchase and remortgage in the UK – Created using data from the Bank of England website[23]

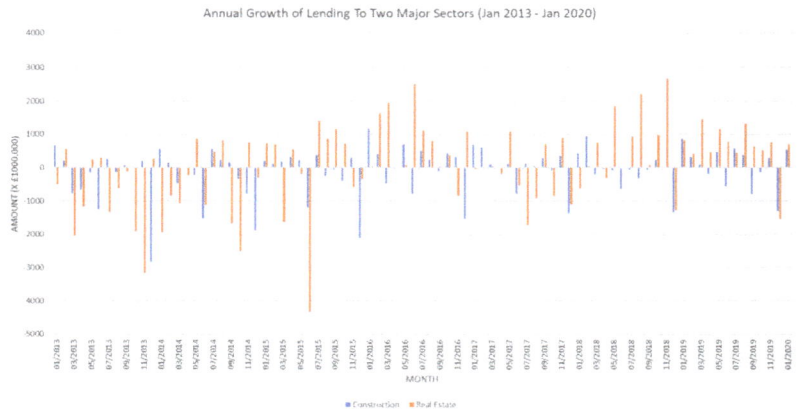

Figure 11.4 Annual growth of lending to construction and real estate in the UK – Created using data from the Bank of England website[24]

Creative Finance Scenario

Let us assume that an investor with capital of £100,000 of their own in their bank account wants to invest in a buy-to-let business. They have two options to select from. The first option is to buy one two-bedroom house using their own capital of £100,000 cash which can achieve a 10% annual yield. Since they are buying this property with cash, they do not need to get a loan so it is a debt-free purchase. The second option is to buy four properties using one mortgage with a 75% loan-to-value for each one. So, their £100,000 will be split over the four properties to pay for their deposits i.e. £25,000 deposit for each property.

Let us compare the achieved income of both purchase options knowing that the investor is using the same amount of capital for the investment, which is £100,000. For option 1, they can aim for a rental income of £10,000 per year i.e. 10% yield. For option 2, they should be able to aim for a gross rental income of £10,000 x 4 which is £40,000. However, they have to pay their monthly mortgage cost (or interest) which is about 3% of the mortgage amount for each of the four properties. This means that their annual income from those four properties will be as follows:

10% Yield – (3% interest rate of four mortgage loans) =
(£10,000 x 4) – 3% x (£75,000 x 4) =
£40,000 – £9,000 = £ 31,000

So, the income generated from the capital investment of buying four properties i.e. using option 2 is £31,000. Making use of good debt/a mortgage to buy the four properties results in a higher annual income that is about three times the income produced from investing all cash in one property. In terms of capital gain, the value of the first options property will be £105,000 at the end of the year. However, if the investor selects the second option of buying four properties instead, the value of the four properties combined will become £420,000 after one year. Therefore, they can make £20,000 on the second option and a gain of only £5,000 on the first option purchase. Figure 11.5 shows a comparison between a cash buyer investment and using a mortgage to buy four income-producing properties.

> Making use of good debt/a mortgage to buy the four properties results in a higher annual income that is about three times the income produced from investing all cash in one property.

Option 1 – cash purchase	Financing comparison		Option 2 – using mortgage
	Cash	Purchase	Mortgage (75%)
£100,000	Price	£100,000 x 4 = £400,000
£0	Loan Amount	£75,000 x 4 = £300,000
£100,000	Capital	£100,000
10% (£10,000)	Achieved annual cashflow	£31,000
5% (£5,000)	Capital gain	5% (£5,000 x 4 = £20,000)

Figure 11.5 Comparison between a cash purchase and using a mortgage

The investor should be able to aim for 20% as a return on capital investment of their £100,000 using option 2. Using good debt/a mortgage to buy more properties results not only in a higher annual income but in a higher return on investment as well. The achieved annual income and return on investment from investing in the four properties is £31,000 + £20,000 = £51,000 which comes from what is known as financial leverage. So, even if the investor does not achieve a good capital gain of 5%, they will still be able to produce £31,000 from rental income which is an excellent achievement anyway.

Leverage refers to the funds received from a lender i.e. debt financing relative to the part financed by equity and measured using the loan-to-value (LTV) ratio. The LTV ratio is defined by how much the lender is willing to fund the purchase of the investment property. Lenders are often reluctant to increase the LTV above a certain level to keep risk under control. Despite the increasing returns from leverage, there is a direct relationship between an investor's leverage and risk. Therefore, property investors should trade off the risk that is brought by leverage with the increased returns achieved by extra lending. The next chapter covers more details about mortgage deposits and LTV ratio.

> Leverage refers to the funds received from a lender i.e. debt financing relative to the part financed by equity and measured using the loan-to-value (LTV) ratio.

Summary

Investors can use creative finance to benefit from certain market conditions, make the right investment decisions, and generate high revenues from rental income as well as capital growth. The main idea of creative finance is for investors to arrange a deal to finance properties using funds from a third-party entity to build an income-producing portfolio and accumulate valuable assets. This chapter has showed how investors use intelligent financial techniques to carry out investment activities and leveraging to expand their portfolios without using much of their own capital. Practical examples of how investors can leverage and expand their income-producing portfolios have been introduced as well.

The way investors raise funds and identify deals such as BMV or distressed properties using capital offered by lenders through mortgage/remortgage products with appropriate LTV has been presented in this chapter. However, using creative finance requires attention and skills in terms of understanding the costs associated with mortgages and debt management. The next chapter will introduce the issue of managing mortgage debts and how to make sure that the associated costs with mortgages are under control. This enables losses to be minimised and keeps the risk of failure as low as possible. Banks do carry out checks on the credit history of potential borrowers and their affordability to make sure they can meet the mortgage conditions and financial commitments. Therefore, the issue of credit referencing, credit reports, using credit cards, and the difference between money, currency, and credit will be introduced.

Managing Debt and Credit Referencing 12

Mortgage debt and its associated costs should always be under control and well managed by investors. Therefore, various aspects of mortgage debt management to minimise risk will be presented in the beginning of this chapter. To minimise losses, banks carry out checks on investors' affordability and credit history to make sure they are capable of paying their financial commitments. This chapter covers credit referencing and discusses how banks use credit reports to gather information and assess the financial status of potential borrowers. Credit reference agencies play a major role in compiling credit reports. Later, the issues of credit referencing, credit reports, and using credit cards by borrowers to pay for products or services will be presented. Credit cards are useful not only to perform financial transactions but also to minimise the risk of carrying out fraudulent transactions.

It has been recognised that money is a standard measure of value for goods and services provided and used for financial transactions. Anyone seeking creative finance skills needs to understand the difference between money, currency, and credit as part of their investment journey, and how banks can influence their investment decisions. At the end of this chapter, the difference between money, currency, and credit is highlighted.

Managing Debt

Real estate investors use debt in order to fund their investment projects and leverage but they have to pay it back within a certain period. Banks are willing to lend to investors by offering different mortgage products with interest to buy properties. Interest is the cost of debt that is offered as a percentage of the money borrowed from the bank.

Investors should know how to manage their investments and borrowed funds, make sure that their debt is under control and avoid bankruptcy. Bankruptcy is a declaration by an individual or company that they are unable to meet their financial commitments and debt repayment. This could have an impact on the investor's reputation, credit rating, future lending, and consequently their investment projects. Therefore, investors have to make sure that the cost of their debt is always less than the income produced by the asset purchased.

Investors should know how to manage their investments and borrowed funds, make sure that their debt is under control and avoid bankruptcy.

Good Debt

- Investing in assets such as real estate

Bad Debt

- Buying liabilities such as expensive TV or car

Figure 12.1 Good debt versus bad debt

In the UK, traditional banks are regulated by the Financial Conduct Authority (FCA) and required to be stringent about their funding and lending criteria. Non-bank financial institutions (NBFIs) do not have a full banking licence and are not regulated by the FCA but offer various banking services such as money transfer, financial consulting, and investment. However, they are not allowed to accept deposits from the public. NBFIs tend to serve as competitors to traditional banks. NBFIs are more flexible in terms of lending criteria to investors or businesses and sometimes offer even better products. Examples of NBFIs include:

> Non-bank financial institutions (NBFIs) do not have a full banking licence and are not regulated by the FCA but offer various banking services such as money transfer, financial consulting, and investment.

- Insurance firms – regulated by the PRA (Prudential Regulation Authority)
- Peer-to-peer lenders
- Crowdfunding
- Commercial loan providers

All banks are required to carry out checks on investors' financial ability and their financial history. This is to make sure that they can provide the deposit that is a percentage of the property price and they are capable of paying their monthly mortgage commitments. Banks often use two main criteria to carry out their checks, as follows:

- Affordability: To check the investor's income, financial commitments, and the house price to earnings ratio
- Credit history: To check the investor's credit card(s) activity, financial transactions, and history using some credit referencing tools

In the UK, high street banks don't lend when an investor's property portfolio reaches a certain level. Property investors with about six to ten properties will face difficulty in getting funding from high street banks for their next property investment. However, non-high street banks such as Precise, Aldermore, The Mortgage Works, LendInvest, Paragon, etc. are often useful options for funding investment projects. As mentioned earlier, NBFIs are more flexible in their lending criteria. Regardless of the number of mortgages someone has, banks use stress testing plus other measures to check whether or not they meet their criteria and to ensure their affordability. Investors only need to look for the best mortgage deal; often their mortgage

> Regardless of the number of mortgages someone has, banks use stress testing plus other measures to check whether or not they meet their criteria and to ensure their affordability.

advisor should be able to offer them a few options and then they can select the best one(s).

It is important to look for mortgages with the smallest interest rates but investors need to check if there are any other fees set by the lender(s). Mortgages with low interest rates tend to incorporate higher fees and vice versa. Bridge loans tend to offer high interest rates and are used to purchase properties at auction but investors only get them from specialist lenders. The offered interest rates by commercial banks are strongly dependent on the base rate decided by the central bank which, in turn, depends on the cyclical phase of the economy. The interest rate is considered as the price paid by the property buyer for the offered mortgage by the bank/lender. Mortgage interest rates affect the property market and prices.

Regardless of whether cheap or expensive mortgages are offered by lenders, banks would expect an investor to contribute to the property price. Moreover, banks would like to make sure that the property produces a good net cash flow. In other words, the rental income paid by tenants should cover the monthly mortgage payment by around 1.3 debt coverage i.e. the monthly rental income is 1.3 times more than the monthly mortgage payment. Investors need to make sure that the property they are buying meets this important requirement. When interest rates are low, this encourages buyers and/or investors to buy properties which increases demand and eventually results in an increase in property prices.

We would expect property developers to respond to the opportunity of cheaper access to credit. The lower interest rates offered by lenders and increased demand for properties will encourage developers to improve the property supply. However, it often takes time for development projects to complete and for newly developed properties to become available to the market. Making proper use of good debt can make a difference in property investment. When capital and mortgages are used wisely, they can increase the annual income and return on investment. The debt used to invest in real estate is often secured against the property an investor is buying. However, using debt increases the risk of their investment as well.

Credit Referencing

Credit referencing refers to gathering information about an individual's financial status including details about their credit score and past track record with credit. Banks use a credit rating system to assess the ability of a potential borrower to meet their financial obligations. To achieve that, they use the borrower's credit report to make their decisions on whether or not to lend to them and how much to lend. An individual's credit report is compiled by companies known as credit reference agencies (CRAs). There are four main CRAs in the UK:

- Experian
- Equifax
- TransUnion
- Crediva

CRAs create and keep hold of people's credit reports. They collect and collate information about their current financial status and credit history.

Each agency holds different information about individuals and produces a credit report that includes a credit score for them based on the information collected. Banks tend to ask one or more CRA agencies for information about individuals before accepting their request for funds. Banks tend to check investors' reports for any existing loans, unpaid or late credit card transactions, mortgage payments, and/or any unclear transactions that can affect their credit rating.

Investors have to check their credit history and score regularly and make sure they take all required measures to improve their credit rating if necessary. There are various useful tools, web applications, and mobile apps that can help individuals to monitor their credit scores and get advice on how to improve their reports. Credit Karma is one of the mobile apps that provides individuals with free access to their credit scores and reports from TransUnion and Equifax. It offers updates on credit reports regularly and allows individuals to track their credit history changes and scores over time.

Checkmyfile.com is an online multi-agency credit report provider which is able to gather information from all four CRAs, as seen in figure 12.2. Checkmyfile.com allows individuals to see their information from the four CRA agencies, and provides a view of an individual's credit scores. So, people can keep an eye on what's being reported about them. All those tools provide useful information and tips to individuals to improve their credit scores in the following ways:

- Make all payments on time
- Check that they are on the electoral register at their current address
- Keep their credit accounts active
- Avoid credit overutilisation and multiple credit applications in a short space of time
- Manage debt and all types of accounts including credit cards, mortgages, loans, etc.

> Banks tend to check investors' reports for any existing loans, unpaid or late credit card transactions, mortgage payments, and/or
>
> There are various useful tools, web applications, and mobile apps that can help individuals to monitor their credit scores and get advice on how to improve their reports.

Figure 12.2 checkmyfile.com

Credit Cards

Credit cards allow individuals to borrow money from a bank, which they can then use within a certain limit to pay for products or services. Credit cards are issued by banks and can be used as an interest-free loan for a limited period or flexible borrowing service. They can be used for payment without any actual money having to be paid upfront, hence allowing cardholders to raise capital for free. For example, experienced property investors know how to use multiple credit cards to pay for property deposits during times when access to cash is limited. Two or three credit cards, depending on their credit limit, can be used to pay for the deposit of a particular property deal that requires quick action. A few more credit cards can be used to pay off the debt of those existing credit cards in the following months to avoid interest charges.

It is one of the skills mastered by very few investors to get funds from third-party institutions to finance their investment projects and build their portfolios. This can be a tricky process of payment as it requires a lot of attention and careful planning and management, to avoid late payments, and consequently any issues in one's credit report and scores. Any late payments of the debt would lead to high interest charges and could have a knock-on effect on the following payments, and consequently on the investor's credit report. Lenders are reluctant to approve mortgages to applicants with a significant level of outstanding debt. As mentioned earlier, they will take a look at a borrower's credit report and history to minimise risk.

> Lenders are reluctant to approve mortgages to applicants with a significant level of outstanding debt.

Credit cardholders are protected and can recover their money between the value of £100–£30,000 under Section 75 of the Consumer Credit Act when purchases go wrong. Some credit card providers offer extra purchase protection above the standard cover. However, you are not protected in all cases so there are situations where you may not be able to claim a refund. As long as the balance is fully paid off and the agreed credit limit is not exceeded, no interest charges will be incurred. However, interest would build up on any unpaid amount. If the borrower chooses to repay only the credit card's minimum payment each month just to avoid a fine, interest will build upon the remaining unpaid balance.

One of the useful features of using a credit card is that cardholders can claim their money back if the product/service has not been delivered by the supplier, service provider, or merchant. However, cardholders should make sure that they use credit cards responsibly, in stages i.e. one project after the other, and for building cash flow and capital. Also, credit card users should always check their monthly credit card statements. This is to determine whether their card has been used by a fraudster to make purchases in their name or carried out fraudulent transactions. Figure 12.3 shows the credit card transaction process.

> One of the useful features of using a credit card is that cardholders can claim their money back if the product/service has not been delivered by the supplier, service provider, or merchant.

A 0% balance transfer credit card allows a cardholder to move an existing debt from one credit card supplier to another. It is a useful way to manage existing debt. Investors have to monitor their credit card activities. Improving credit card activity will encourage banks to send cardholders offers for finance and increase their balance limit to a larger amount. They control the credit limit, annual fee, and interest rate. Cardholders have to manage their credit card properly and make sure that they stick to the rules otherwise they may get into financial difficulty and unnecessary trouble. Also, cardholders and investors, in particular, have to make sure that they play the game carefully otherwise the outcome is painful. Credit cards are useful for:

- Short-term financing
- Building a credit history
- Buying products and services but most importantly buying assets

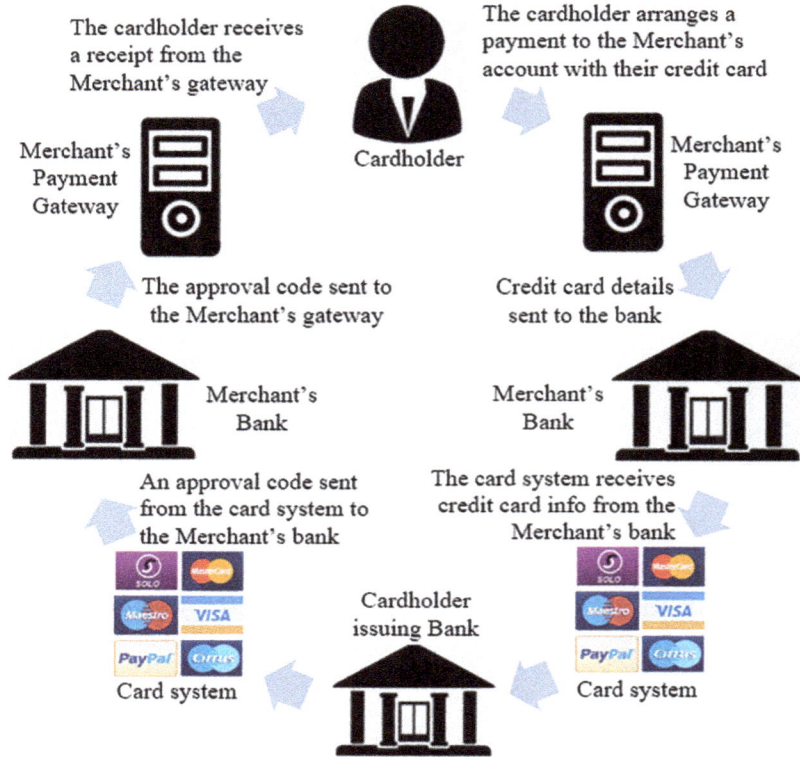

Figure 12.3 Credit card transaction process

Money, Currency, and Credit

Money is a lubricant that plays a major role in keeping investors moving forward and allowing the flow of wealth around the globe. It has been recognised by the world community as a standard measure of value for goods and services provided as well as for daily financial transactions. Money is used by economists to measure the purchasing power of people and control price stability. Be aware that investors do not work for money; their money works for them. Today money is issued by central banks in a physical or digital form and deposited by people in their bank accounts. Gold is considered good money whereas currency is referred to as bad money.

Currency is not a safe store of value and can lose its value because of various reasons and circumstances, such as inflation and economic downturn, among other factors. Active investors know what makes real money;

Money is used by economists to measure the purchasing power of people and control price stability.

that is why they know where to invest and store their money if necessary. This will not only protect their asset wealth but also ensure that the value of their assets increases. During the 20th century, new methods of money transaction emerged such as electronic payments, digital money, online transactions, and using credit cards. However, although both money and credit offer purchasing power to people, they are different. The following table highlights the major differences between money and credit.

During the 20th century, new methods of money transaction emerged such as electronic payments, digital money, online transactions, and using credit cards.

Money	Credit
Physical money in the form of coins and notes that are used as a medium of exchange	Virtual money in the form of credit cards or loans but can be converted into cash
Maintained by people and banks as physical cash	Offered by banks to people in the form of loans with interest i.e. not free
Accessible cash to buy goods and services	Accessible money through credit cards or loans
Used by a limited number of customers who withdraw cash and consumed on a daily basis	The majority of credit transfers use electronic transactions
A lot of cash is required to buy expensive goods and/or services	You do not need to have a lot of cash to buy expensive goods and/or services
No extra costs or interest by using your money or savings/debit account	There is a cost associated with using credit until it is paid back
There is no limit to using your money	There is a limit to using credit

Table 12.1 Distinction between money and credit

Summary

Creative finance can help investors to raise funds, however it requires certain skills such as a good understanding of how to manage mortgage debts and any other costs associated with raising capital. Banks do have their own procedures to check the credit reports and history of investors and assess their financial status and affordability. This is to make sure the borrower is able to pay their monthly mortgage payments during the full term of the mortgage and keep the risk of lending as minimal as possible. This chapter introduced the issue of debt management and how banks carry out their checks on potential borrowers and their financial status to minimise risk. Investors need to understand financial-related matters such as credit referencing, using credit cards, and the difference between money, currency, and credit, all of which have been presented in this chapter.

Another important skill necessary for investors is property accounting and how financial statements including profit and loss reports and balance sheets are prepared. The next chapter will introduce property accounting which is important for producing and reporting accurate financial statements resulting from investment operations. The use of accounting software and tools such as Xero should help investors to manage their accounts, access financial transactions as well as project their future profits. Various issues about business operating and non-operating expenses, property tax considerations, and filing tax reports at the end of each tax year will also be discussed in the next chapter.

Accounting Considerations

13

Accounting is the process of producing, summarising, and reporting financial records and transactions resulting from business operations over a specified period. Organising business accounts is key to managing real estate financial transactions and records as well as preparing financial statements. This chapter introduces the concepts and principles of property accounting and the importance of accurate accounting in property investment. It covers financial statements including profit and loss reports and balance sheets produced using accounting software known as Xero. Xero has been presented because we use it at Anzar Property Group but there is other accounting software available to support businesses. With proper planning and understanding of their financial situation, investors should be able to develop accurate projections for their future revenues, expenses, and tax commitments. Investors have to file their tax reports at the end of each tax year, so the main types of property tax are presented at the end of this chapter.

Property Accounting

An important aspect of any business in general and real estate, in particular, is to ensure that financial records and income reports are accurate and comply with tax laws. The produced reports are not only important to the management of the investment operations and decision making but also to lenders, investors, employees, and government. The accounting records are important because they show the current financial status of the business, how the business is progressing, and how profitable it is. Financial accounting is concerned with:

> The accounting records are important because they show the current financial status of the business, how the business is progressing, and how profitable it is.

- Designing all the internal controls necessary for management and auditing
- Developing a system for analysing the data recorded from bookkeeping and minimising errors
- Recording transactions, developing financial reports, and measuring out revenues and expenses for a business to determine profits and losses during a particular period
- Analysing data from bookkeeping to report the business financial results, financial statements, tax returns, and performance measures

Real estate investors need to make sure that they have an accurate view of the financial situation of their business and it is reported to them regularly. Accounting reports are very useful in helping business owners to develop their financial strategy and to make important financial decisions whenever necessary. Another aspect of the accounting business is bookkeeping which is used to support accounting activities and operations. Bookkeeping is an important aspect of the real estate investment operations which complements the accounting business. It is the process of tracking, gathering, organising, and recording business financial transactions and activities. Bookkeeping is important for the preparation of financial reports (e.g. profits and expenses) and tax returns.

Financial Statements

Financial statements are important documents required by the HMRC (Her Majesty's Revenue and Customs) to show off different financial information about the business and to maintain its transparency. Such documents are often requested by lenders to check how the business is performing before granting funds to investment projects. The two main financial statements are:

I. profit and loss statement and
II. balance sheet

> A profit and loss statement is a document required to report a company's financial status and performance over a specific period.

A profit and loss statement is a document required to report a company's financial status and performance over a specific period. As part of the company's annual report, it provides a summary of how the company will incur its revenues and expenses or the net loss and net profit. Also, it provides information about the company's earnings before it pay taxes. For example, the profit and loss statement in a buy-to-let property business is divided into four parts as follows:

1. **Operating expenses:** provides information about the costs that come from regular business activity such as initial refurbishment, building insurance, and repairs

2. **Non-operating expenses:** provide information about the costs that do not come directly from regular business activity such as accountancy fees, marketing, and training

3. **Gross profit** = revenue − operating expenses

4. **Net profit** = revenue − (operating + non-operating expenses). If the outcome is negative, then the investor will have a net loss. Net profit is the most common indicator of how profitable the business is.

Notice that the net profit produced on the profit and loss statement is before tax. It is often useful to show the profit and loss figures as a percent of the rental income because it is easy to:

- Analyse the statement including all revenue and expenses figures
- Compare how the business is performing in comparison to previous years
- Manage losses and identify which of the costs make up the biggest portion of the income

Profit and Loss Statement

Figure 13.1 shows a sample of a profit and loss statement for a property investment company. Accounting software called Xero is used to generate this profit and loss statement. Figure 13.2 shows a Xero dashboard for a business account. There are different tools available on the market that are used to produce financial statements and reports. Xero is well-known online accounting software used by business companies to:

- Manage financial accounts and monitor their business health
- Import bank transactions, send invoice reminders, and automatically handle tasks so businesses can get their accounts completed and reported accurately
- View net profit and cash flow in a real-time manner
- Create professional invoices, calculate payroll, pay employees, and manage taxes
- Chase outstanding payments with automated reminders

	Property1	Property2	Property3	.....	Proeprty28	Property29	Property30	Business	Unassigned	Total
Profit and Loss Limited Company 1 June 2019 to May 2020										
Income										
Rental Income	£9,000.00	£7,800.00	£9,600.00	.....	£8,750.00	£8,760.00	£11,400.00	£0.00	£0.00	£274,750
Total Income	£9,000.00	£7,800.00	£9,600.00	.....	£8,750.00	£8,760.00	£11,400.00	£0.00	£0.00	£274,750
Less Cost of Sales										
Ground Rent & Service Charge	£155.17	£476.22	£499.70	.....	£45.00	£836.79	£775.56	£0.00	£0.00	£8,796.78
Initial Refurbishment (like for like)	£2,750.61	£0.00	£883.39		£0.00	£54.60	£0.00	£0.00	£531.92	£12,730.54
Insurance	£36.15	£17.95	£317.95		£176.45	£297.90	£194.55	£0.00	£0.00	£6,231.64
Letting Agent Fees	£0.00	£0.00	£350.00		£0.00	£0.00	£0.00	£0.00	£0.00	£650
Mortgages Interest Only	£2,328.88	£2,537.44	£2,082.10		£4,245.72	£3,911.70	£2,794.32	£0.00	£229.96	£92,679.57
Property Repairs & Maintenance	£0.00	£0.00	£673.88		£146.00	£375.97	£53.00	£14.99	£9.50	£4,468.52
Utilities	£35.00	£0.00	£0.00	.....	£0.00	£0.00	£0.00	£0.00	£0.00	£156.82
Total Cost of Sales	£5,305.81	£3,031.61	£4,797.02	.....	£4,613.17	£5,476.96	£3,817.43	£14.99	£771.38	£125,713.87
Gross Profit	£3,694.19	£4,768.39	£4,802.98	.....	£4,136.83	£3,283.04	£7,582.57	-£14.99	-£771.38	£149,036.13
Less Operating Expenses										
Advertising & Marketing	£0.00	£0.00	£29.00		£0.00	£350.00	£0.00	£1,798.07	£0.00	£3,177.07
Audit & Accountancy fees	£0.00	£0.00	£0.00		£0.00	£0.00	£0.00	£1,744.68	£0.00	1,944.68
Bank Fees	£0.00	£10.00	£150.00		£0.00	£0.00	£10.00	£266.00	£21.71	258.71
Consulting	£0.00	£0.00	£0.00		£0.00	£0.00	£0.00	£21.00	£0.00	£41
Council Tax	£5.00	£0.00	£90.34		£47.97	£45.47	£0.00	£0.00	£0.00	£621.30
General Expenses	£0.00	£0.00	£0.00		£0.00	£0.00	£0.00	£43.07	£0.00	£83.07
Legal Fees	£0.00	£0.00	£0.00		£0.00	£50.00	£0.00	£340.00	£0.00	629.49
Light, Power, Heating	£0.00	£0.00	£39.95		£0.00	£11.07	£0.00	£0.00	£0.00	£186.02
Postage, Freight & Courier	£0.00	£0.00	£6.60		£0.00	£0.00	£0.00	£0.00	£0.00	£33.20
Salaries	£0.00	£0.00	£0.00		£0.00	£0.00	£0.00	£0.00	£21,366.66	£61,366.66
Staff Training	£0.00	£0.00	£0.00		£0.00	£0.00	£0.00	£160.31	£0.00	£10,060.31
Subscriptions	£0.00	£0.00	£0.00		£0.00	£0.00	£0.00	£977.28	£190.00	1167.28
Telephone & Internet	£0.00	£0.00	£0.00		£0.00	£0.00	£0.00	£41.48	£0.00	£141.48
Travel & Subsistence	£10.48	£0.00	£210.58		£0.00	£78.45	£0.00	£48.51	£6.35	£569.52
Total Operating Expenses	£15.48	£10.00	£527.07	.....	£47.97	£534.99	£10.00	£5,440.40	£21,584.72	£80,279.79
Net Profit	£3,678.71	£4,758.39	£4,275.91	.....	£4,088.86	£2,748.05	£7,572.57	-£5,455.39	-£22,356.10	£68,756.34

Figure 13.1 Profit and loss statement

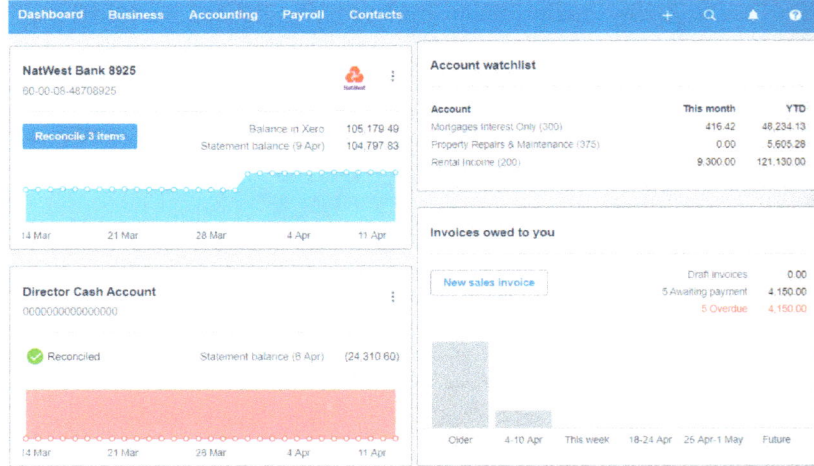

Figure 13.2 Accounts dashboard in Xero

Balance Sheet

A balance sheet is a financial statement that includes the following three important pieces of information about a business:

I. A company's assets e.g. all business BTL (buy-to-let properties), cash or cash equivalents
II. A company's liabilities e.g. total mortgage values and
III. Shareholder(s) or owner's equity

The balance sheet provides a clear snapshot of the financial state of the company in terms of its capital owned and debt using the following formula:

$$Owner's\ equity = Assets - Liabilities$$

The balance sheet is used to evaluate its financial structure and to perform financial analysis at a particular point in time. It is an important document that is used to value a particular business and helps in terms of how the outside world views the business. Banks often ask for such a document to check if the business is in a good financial position, to establish what debts and/or financial obligations the company has, and whether or not to fund the investment project. Having a profitable business but with great debts is not an issue, as long as the business can show a healthy financial status and generate good profits.

Banks and investors like to receive a detailed balance sheet to help them make the right decisions. It is useful to use the balance sheet as part of an investor pack to attract potential investors so that they are happy to fund investment projects or can join current or future joint venture projects. Figure 13.3 shows an example of a summarised balance sheet for a property company that is produced using Xero software. Notice that the company's main business is in BTL and the balance sheet does not include any cash available in the company's accounts. According to the provided figures, the owner's equity can be calculated as follows.

> The balance sheet is used to evaluate its financial structure and to perform financial analysis at a particular point in time.

Owner's equity = £4,782,000 – £2,777,632 = £2,004,368

Property address	Year Built	Original Purchase Price	No. Of bedrooms	Tenure	Current Property Value	Current Mortgage Balance	Monthly Payment	Rental Income
Property 1	1975	£100,000	3	Freehold	£165,000	£76,501	£334.05	£750
Property 2	1975	£78,000	2	Freehold	£135,000	£71,550	£210.18	£650
Property 3	1975	£78,000	3	Freehold	£175,000	£92,245	£261.08	£800
Property 4	2008	£124,000	3	Leasehold	£185,000	£131,250	£413.44	£950
Property 5	2004	£99,000	3	Leasehold	£165,000	£107,495	£303.99	£875
Property 6	2003	£88,000	3	Leasehold	£170,000	£103,753	£293.62	£825
Property 7	1982	£33,000	2	Leasehold	£135,000	£77,177	£187.30	£675
Property 8	1998	£98,000	3	Leasehold	£175,000	£103,639	£293.04	£750
Property 9	1993	£30,000	3	Freehold	£160,000	£76,639	£183.75	£725
Property 10	2008	£112,000	3	Leasehold	£195,000	£114,766	£277.31	£825
Property 11	2008	£101,500	3	Freehold	£175,000	£108,750	£342.56	£925
Property 12	1998	£69,000	2	Leasehold	£135,000	£76,991	£187.04	£625
Property 13	2012	£138,000	3	Leasehold	£185,000	£111,504	£361.46	£950
Property 14	2003	£85,000	2	Leasehold	£120,000	£68,680	£222.64	£650
Property 15	2003	£86,250	2	Leasehold	£120,000	£66,237	£181.79	£650
Property 16	2012	£155,000	4	Leasehold	£210,000	£125,240	£416.42	£1,200
Property 17	1999	£121,500	3	Leasehold	£175,000	£83,300	£535.69	£850
Property 18	2008	£153,000	4	Leasehold	£210,000	£142,500	£484.50	£950
Property 19	1999	£105,000	2	Leasehold	£135,000	£90,000	£306.00	£650
Property 20	1999	£105,000	2	Leasehold	£135,000	£80,281	£233.88	£700
Property 21	1999	£110,500	3	Leasehold	£165,000	£82,820	£532.60	£825
Property 22	2005	£128,000	3	Freehold	£195,000	£116,250	£372.00	£850
Property 23	1999	£115,000	3	Leasehold	£165,000	£116,250	£395.25	£800
Property 24	1999	£90,000	2	Leasehold	£135,000	£67,500	£353.81	£700
Property 25	1999	£105,000	2	Leasehold	£135,000	£79,926	£232.86	£700
Property 26	1999	£110,000	2	Leasehold	£135,000	£88,880	£288.12	£700
Property 27	2000	£115,500	2	Leasehold	£130,000	£75,734	£210.14	£750
Property 28	2003	£120,000	2	Leasehold	£132,000	£76,438	£267.45	£730
Property 29	2008	£122,350	2	Leasehold	£135,000	£79,356	£280.56	£725
Property 30	2000	£145,000	3	Leasehold	£195,000	£85,980	£342.16	£950
Total		£3,120,600			£4,782,000	£2,777,632	£9,305	£23,705

Figure 13.3 A summarised balance sheet/property portfolio

For a real estate business, the balance sheets represent the company or investor's property portfolio. Some of the property portfolio details are already available on the Companies House and Land Registry websites. Whenever investors ask their mortgage advisor for mortgage options to refinance or buy a property, investors expect their advisors to ask for an updated copy of their portfolio regardless of its size. This allows them to send a copy of the portfolio to potential lenders. After the 2008 global financial crisis, lenders have become stricter with their lending criteria and procedures and ask investors to provide their up-to-date portfolios whenever they ask for funds or remortgage loans.

This property portfolio represents a useful real-life case study. For example, property 9 was bought relatively cheaply for £30,000, which was then refinanced by the company which managed to release equity of £76,639 from this property i.e. about double the original price. Amateur investors need to gain the necessary knowledge about refinancing, the power of compounding yields, gearing/leveraging, and good debt. Ex-council derelict properties that are for sale could be a good way to start learning about property investment, especially if they are at the right location e.g. close to a city's CBD or amenities. Often, they are useful for learning the purchase process, legal matters, and renovation skills before renting them

Whenever investors ask their mortgage advisor for mortgage options to refinance or buy a property, investors expect their advisors to ask for an updated copy of their portfolio regardless of its size.

Amateur investors need to gain the necessary knowledge about refinancing, the power of compounding yields, gearing/leveraging, and good debt.

out. Such properties could make good investment opportunities if they are in the right location. They can attract certain communities and may produce good yields. Property investment could be an interesting and enjoyable game but requires attention as well.

In a real estate portfolio, the liabilities are the funds provided by the banks or lenders to support the property investment projects. It is the debt that the company owes to the banks or lenders. The assets are the residential or commercial properties that are used to support the business and to generate income. The generated income could be used to support business operations and/or for reinvestment purposes. The main property business operations are as follows:

- Managing the assets i.e. properties
- Preparing the tenancy agreements
- Arranging building insurance, boiler insurance, gas, and electric safety
- Arranging and managing repair works
- Managing resources

Property Tax

Taxation has been used for many centuries even before the modern state to raise funds, develop its social and economic projects, and to control and manage the state and its economy. It is now used by governments to manage citizens and businesses' expenditure, forecast the economy, and plan for budgets. Regardless of the type of business investors have, they will have to file their taxes before the end of the tax year. Therefore, it is important to have accurate financial statements and accounting records ready for filing these taxes. Real estate investors are required to keep records of their financial transactions and to produce accurate accounts whenever requested by legal entities such as HMRC (HM Revenue & Customs) in the UK.

With the help of their accountants and accurate financial statements, investors should be able to complete their relevant tax forms and make use of applicable deductions. Accurate accounts would help accountants to offset every expense and to take all costs into account. Tax deadlines are strict, so late tax returns are liable to fixed penalties and/or interest charges. Knowing the current financial situation will help investors to develop accurate projections with realistic estimates for their future expenses and tax commitments. With proper financial planning and robust recording systems, real estate investors should be able to predict their future rental income and revenues.

Real estate investors should be able to manage their capital and forecast their capital position fairly accurately so that they plan early for their financial and tax obligations. In this way they will be able to avoid unexpected payments, overspending, and delayed tax payments. As an employer, any real estate investor should act as a tax collector for the government by maintaining accurate financial records and an effective payroll system for their employees. Simplicity and using quality tax accounting tools and bookkeeping packages play a major role in developing an effective accounting system and tax accounting for their company. Tax accounting is an accounting process that uses complex operations and focuses on:

- Preparing and filing taxes
- Helping investors to track all their financial activities such as incoming funds, expenses, revenues, and business financial obligations
- Reducing tax liabilities, and
- Following the necessary rules to complete tax returns

Governments use systems to collect different types of tax. In the UK, HMRC is the tax, payment, and custom authority. According to HMRC, they have the authority to

"collect the money that pays for the UK's public services and help families and individuals with targeted financial support" and

"help the honest majority to get their tax right and make it hard for the dishonest minority to cheat the system."

Figure 13.4 shows the homepage of HMRC. The following sections will introduce some of the tax systems imposed by HMRC.

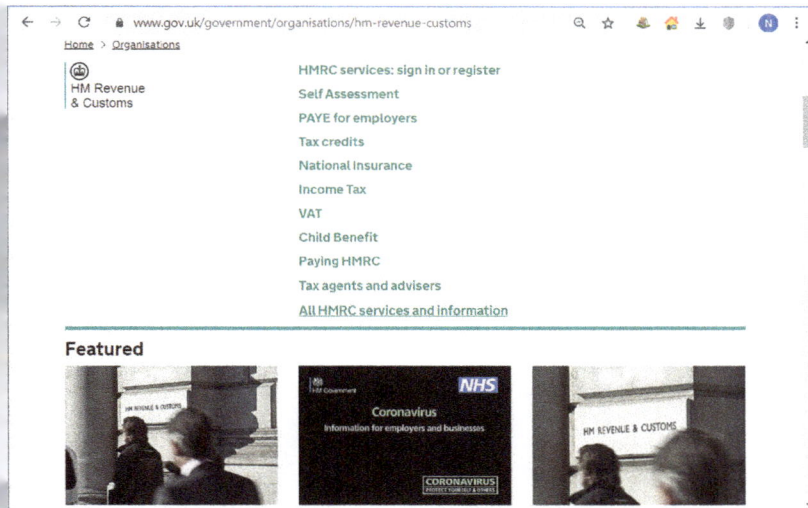

Figure 13.4 HM Revenue & Customs homepage

Income Tax

Property investors in the BTL business are required to complete a tax return under the rules of "Residential Lettings". As part of their personal income and their company's business income, rental income tax cannot be offset against income earned from other jobs. They might be able to claim tax relief on their business expenses. These expenses are set out by HMRC. For some claims, they must keep records e.g. receipts of what they have spent. According to HMRC, "Income Tax is a tax you pay on your income. You do not have to pay tax on all types of income."

The income tax collected by HMRC depends on a tax allowance and a tax rate. An allowance is the amount of income that investors are allowed to earn, and do not have to pay income tax on i.e. non-taxable income.

> An allowance is the amount of income that investors are allowed to earn, and do not have to pay income tax on i.e. non-taxable income.

However, they must pay tax at the applicable tax rate on all taxable income above the non-taxable earning i.e. their personal allowance. The tax rate determines the percentage that investors have to pay to HMRC. As their income increases, the percentage that they have to pay as tax increases. Table 13.1 lists the taxable income and rate. The current tax system only has three bands. Another form of income tax by the government is the National Insurance Contribution (NIC) which is deducted by anyone in employment.

Taxable income	Rate
Non-taxable income (Up to £12,500)	0%
Basic rate (£12,500-£50,000)	20%
Higher rate (£50,000-£150,000)	40%
Additional rate (Over £150,000)	45%

Table 13.1 Taxable income and rate – Source: https://www.gov.uk/income-tax-rates

Stamp Duty

Another type of tax that is collected by the government to manage its public finance and budget is Stamp Duty Land Tax (SDLT), as mentioned previously. In England, SDLT is the main tax on property transactions that must be paid if an investor buys a property or land over a specific price. It is a tax that they will pay when buying a property or land costing an extra amount. For residential properties, the current SDLT threshold is £125,000 and for buy-to-let properties, they must pay SDLT regardless of the property price. However, there are different SDLT rules if an investor is buying their first home. Legally, it is their responsibility to make sure that their stamp duty/transaction tax is paid before the deadline set by the government. The tax rate that they need to pay varies depending on the property price as follows:

> In England, SDLT is the main tax on property transactions that must be paid if an investor buys a property or land over a specific price.

BUY-TO-LET Stamp Duty Rates

Property Purchase Price	Buy-To-Let	Standard Rate
Up to £125,000	3%	0%
£125,001 - £250,000	5%	2%
£250,001 - £925,000	8%	5%
£925,001 - £1.5 million	13%	10%
Over £1.5 million	15%	12%

Figure 13.5 Created using data from gov.uk website[25]

Here is an example:

An investor is planning to buy a buy-to-let property for £500,000. They will have to pay 3% on the first £125,000, 5% on £125,001–£250,000, and 8% on the remaining amount above £250,000.

The SDLT to be paid is:

$$£125,000 \times 3\% = £3,750$$

$$(£250,000 - £125,000) \times 5\% = £6,250$$

$$£150,000 \times 8\% = £12,000$$

Therefore, the SDLT amount to be paid is £22,000.

Capital Gains Tax

Capital Gains Tax (CGT) is paid by an investor or asset owner to the government when they sell the asset (e.g. buy-to-let property) for more than the original price they bought it at and the capital spent on it. The CGT is paid on the capital gained i.e. a tax on the profit when an asset owner sells an "asset" that has increased in value, not the full amount of capital they receive. Not all assets are taxable. Asset owners also do not have to pay CGT if all their gains in a year are below their tax-free allowance. So, they only pay CGT on capital gains above their tax-free allowance i.e. the Annual Exempt Amount. For more details and up-to-date rates check the UK government website https://www.gov.uk/capital-gains-tax.

> The CGT is paid on the capital gained i.e. a tax on the profit when an asset owner sells an "asset" that has increased in value, not the full amount of capital they receive.

Corporation Tax

Corporation Tax is imposed on limited companies' profits and capital gains. It is a legal obligation the investment business owes the government. As a limited company, the business must register for Corporation Tax when it starts doing business and must keep its accounting records up to date. Taxable profits gained from a company business and from which the company must pay Corporation Tax include the income the company managed to make from the following activities:

- Trading business
- Successful investment
- Selling assets for more than they cost i.e. chargeable gains

Check the https://www.gov.uk/corporation-tax website for up-to-date rates and more details.

Summary

All investment businesses require accounting operations and financial accounting knowledge to process their financial data, report their financial records, and file their accounts at the end of each tax year. Real estate investment operations produce various types of financial transactions that require recording and financial accounting. Real estate investors have to understand how property accounting operates and how financial statements including profit and loss statements and balance sheets are prepared. This chapter introduced property accounting and highlighted the importance of recording all financial transactions resulting from property investment operations. Accounting software called Xero can be used by investors to manage their financial transactions and records and produce accurate financial statements.

Running a real estate investment business requires careful management of its operations, finances, and accounts as well as risk analysis. The next chapter introduces the subject of risk management as an important aspect of real estate investment. Investors require the necessary knowledge and understanding of risk analysis for different asset classes to minimise losses and increase the likelihood of positive results. Different levels of risk can have an impact on different investment strategies and asset classes which require accurate risk analysis. The necessary skills to manage risk to keep the likelihood of failure to a minimum and develop risk tolerance to deal with unpleasant scenarios will be discussed in the next chapter.

Risk Management

14

Real estate investment requires careful preparation, research, study, and risk analysis. Risk is the likelihood of losing part or all of your invested money. Therefore, the importance of understanding and analysing risk in real estate investment will be covered first in this chapter. Different asset classes have different levels of risk, but there is no riskless investment. Therefore, risk management is important for property investors to reduce any potential losses and maximise the likelihood of positive outcomes. The main issues of risk management in the real estate business are highlighted next. The aim of risk management is to identify and evaluate the financial risks associated with the business and its earnings and resources.

Real estate investors should acquire the necessary skills required to manage and keep the risk of failure as minimal as possible. They have to be aware of the risk of losing out if their property business does not achieve its predicted profits due to unexpected changes in the market or economic circumstances. Risk tolerance is another issue that investors should consider during their investment journey in order to deal with worst-case scenarios, withstand market fluctuations, and tackle unexpected changes to their revenues. At the end of the chapter, the issue of risk tolerance is introduced.

Risk in Real Estate Investment

Investment risk is the likelihood of incurring financial loss rather than an expected return from a particular investment. Risk management is the process of identifying, forecasting, and evaluating a financial risk that is likely to happen to a business and its earnings and resources. In this way you can minimise the likelihood of potential losses due to various negative reasons and maximise the likelihood of a positive result and events. Investments that promise high income such as a stock market are often considered high risk. Medium risk investments such as property usually provide a steady and medium level of income.

Investments that promise low risk such as bank savings often provide minimum income. Financial risk management is concerned with identifying the types of factors and price fluctuation that have the greatest impact on business value. Figure 14.1 shows the relationship between the three levels of investment risks and returns. The three main levels of investment kinds with different levels of risk are the stock market, real estate, and saving accounts, as follows:

- Stock shares/Equity: Most of the investment literature indicates that investing in stock markets is very risky especially for beginners.

Risk management is the process of identifying, forecasting, and evaluating a financial risk that is likely to happen to a business and its earnings and resources.

- Real estate: Real estate investment has a moderate level of risk. It provides long-term growth and consistent cash flow. Having an income-generating property investment provides security and regular returns.

- Cash savings: With the current rate of inflation being over 2% per annum, cash is slowly being eroded as banks are offering no or very low returns on an individual's cash savings.

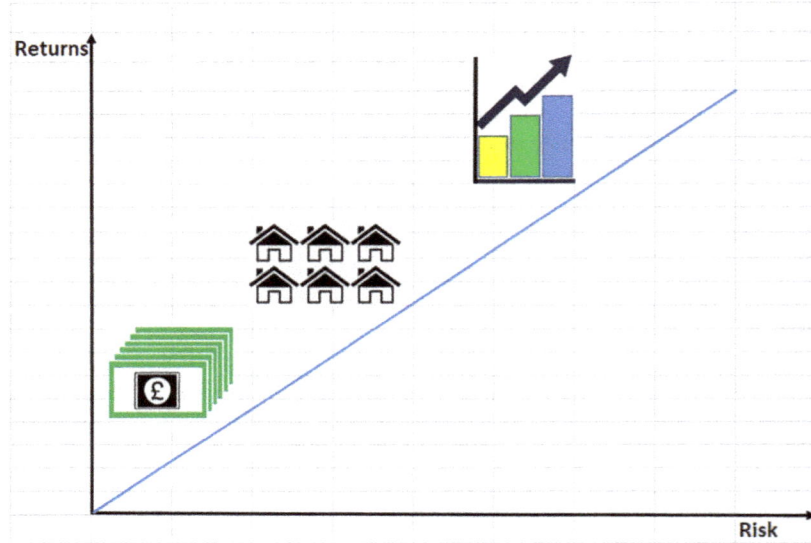

Figure 14.1 Risk vs returns

"Risk comes from not knowing what you are doing."
Warren Buffett

In property investment, an increased value of debt due to deflation has to be considered as part of the risk. Higher debt levels are part of leveraged finance, but debt becomes a problem if the property is unable to maintain a good yield and/or tenants are unable to pay their rents. That is why it is important to make sure that tenants do pass a rigorous affordability check before signing a tenancy agreement. During the COVID-19 pandemic which started in early 2020, furloughed workers were receiving support from the UK government, so the majority of tenants were able to pay their rent.

We witnessed how UK businesses such as the hospitality sector, airlines, and sports industry were struggling. But the situation was different in other businesses such as e-commerce – they were booming during the lockdown. There is always an element of risk and that is the case with any business and/or investment. Real estate investment involves the risk of losing out financially if the portfolio does not achieve its target and produce the expected income. For example, some properties become empty for a long period, or

Higher debt levels are part of leveraged finance, but debt becomes a problem if the property is unable to maintain a good yield and/or tenants are unable to pay their rents.

Real estate investment involves the risk of losing out financially if the portfolio does not achieve its target and produce the expected income.

tenants are unable to pay their rent due to unemployment or unexpected circumstances.

Investors have to be aware of the changes that might happen to the market in terms of supply and demand. Unexpected changes to the market can happen due to various factors and changes to tenants' circumstances can happen because of different reasons. The demand for rentals can go up and down and stock availability can change as well. Likewise, the supply of properties depends on changes in the rental market and changes in demand for residential or commercial properties. The major risks in property investment and development include but are not limited to:

- Unexpected changes to supply and demand
- Increases in tax such as stamp duty, CGT, or income tax which could have a knock-on effect on supply and demand
- Extra costs associated with buying and/or selling investment properties
- Difficulty of selling a property due to high competition and/or time constraints
- Unexpected changes to government rules and/or tax regulations

The major risks of the buy-to-let investment include but are not limited to:

- On-time rent payment is not guaranteed
- Void periods could be unavoidable
- Increased costs associated with ground rent and service charges for leased properties and apartments
- Falling demand
- The increased cost of lending

Risk Management

Risk management is a process that allows investors to identify, evaluate, and mitigate the impact of potential losses. Investors have to keep the effects of such risks when they occur to a minimum. They have to evaluate whatever changes in the market in terms of how it could affect future income from a potential investment. Property investment in general and buy-to-let in particular is a long-term business; therefore, such a business requires a long-term vision and careful planning. As risk-takers, successful property investors are not reluctant to deal with risk and to accept large amounts of capital to fund their investment projects and business activities. They take the risk of setting up property companies, investing a lot of time in acquiring the know-how knowledge to deal with banks, mortgage advisors, solicitors, local authorities, estate agents, insurance, developers, planners, utility service providers, etc.

Active investors are willing to learn marketing, sales, technology, real estate economics, property law, project management, finance, accounting, tax rules, operations management, business strategy, and most importantly understand how to deal with clients and customers. Experienced real estate business investors with many property mortgages would be as concerned about Bank of England interest rate fluctuations as any starting business owner. Therefore, diversifying the business portfolio across different strategies would provide the investor with options to reduce risk.

When an interest rate increases, it will have a significant impact on raising the cost of tracker type of mortgages and new property purchases, while at the same time, revenues and rental yield will decrease. For example, a property investment company that owns and rents many buy-to-let properties might need to use its risk profile to investigate and analyse the business exposure to interest rate fluctuations. The rise in interest rate will increase their monthly mortgage payments and decrease the monthly cashflow income. The investor needs to consider taking certain measures to reduce that exposure, for example by reviewing their rents and monthly expenses regularly, and considering fixed-rate mortgages and/or different investment strategies.

Insurance is a form of risk management by which businesses undertake to transfer the risk of potential financial losses or accidental damages to an insurance service provider in return for a guaranteed compensation. Insurance service providers are willing to take on the risk in return for a premium paid by the insured business. The insurance policy would include all the terms and conditions agreed upon between both parties, the insurance company, and the policyholder or insuree. Without insurance, real estate businesses would be vulnerable to unexpected losses of their investment portfolios, properties, and earnings.

Uninsured investors could become unable to grow and might face bankruptcy in the case of adverse events. For example, properties could be insured against adverse events such as flooding or fire. Banks want to have a building insurance policy in place before they transfer a mortgage loan to a property investor. Investors should make the necessary arrangements to pay a fee to the insurance company in exchange for compensation if an unexpected loss happens. Also, investors have to be aware of the importance of the tenancy rules and regulations including contract agreement. Such issues determine the legal rights and responsibilities of both parties, investors and tenants. The tenancy agreement should specify how much rental income will be received from the tenant.

Investors or landlords should be able to use technology and available tools to support their business and management activities. For example, they can use online banking apps to manage their financial transactions or a tool such as Mileiq to track their mileage and manage travel expenses, etc. They can use online deposit protection services to manage their deposit protection accounts for their tenants. Also, they can use an online service such as the DocuSign eSignature tool to get the tenant to sign the tenancy agreement, as shown in figure 14.2. The tenant should be able to set up their account and use this online service to sign future tenancy agreements. This will speed up the process of signing and exchanging the contracts.

All available tools and functions are important and require proper attention because they can affect the progress of the business and investment. Investors must not only have the skills of buying and selling but also operating, managing real estate business, and making use of technology to deliver a quality service. All such skills and activities are useful to build a successful investment and to keep the risk of failure to a minimum. In the property business, to minimise risk, investors might need to

The rise in interest rate will increase their monthly mortgage payments and decrease the monthly cashflow income.

Investors should make the necessary arrangements to pay a fee to the insurance company in exchange for compensation if an unexpected loss happens.

- Acquire the necessary knowledge of management, finance, and technology
- Actively assess the market and adapt to changes
- Think about diversifying their business portfolio in different types of property investments such as REITs, HMOs or service accommodation, etc.
- Be accredited by the industry's key governing bodies such as NRLA, IoD (for company directors)
- Attend property investment events such as seminars, workshops, and network meetings
- Think about investing in different regions and/or even countries if appropriate
- Learn budgeting for contingencies
- Develop an exit strategy to minimise losses

*"The only strategy that is guaranteed to
fail is not taking any risks."*
Mark Zuckerberg

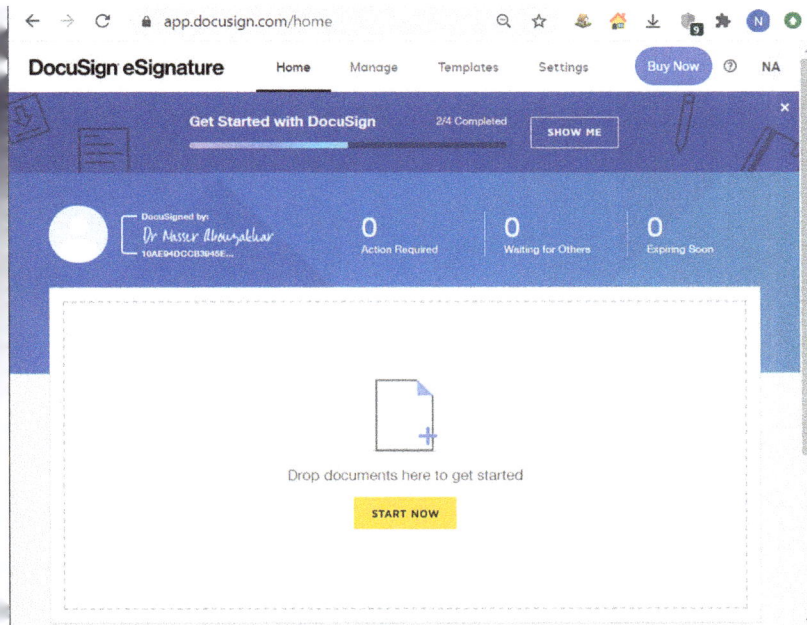

Figure 14.2 DocuSign, an online e-signature tool

Risk Tolerance and Mitigation

Risk tolerance is another issue that investors need to be aware of. It is about an investor's ability to withstand market fluctuation and to deal with changes in investment returns. Real estate investors have to deal with all scenarios and review worst-case scenarios and situations to be able to predict future losses during bad times. This requires a regular assessment of their short-term and long-term circumstances and financial situation. Loss of initial investment, reduced rental demand, increased interest rates, increased inflation, and rental voids are examples of investment risks.

The idea behind risk tolerance is to make investors ready for the unexpected, determine which investment best suits them, and assess how much they are willing to lose. Regardless of the investment type or asset class, investors have to improve their risk knowledge, understand risk tolerance, and how to assess their tolerance to risk. Different asset classes can be affected by different levels of risk. BTL investment has a medium risk but investing in REITs is a medium to high risk. Figure 14.3 shows the change in property prices from 1970 to 2020. Property prices tend to change due to various factors and market situation. During the 2008 credit crunch, the rate of unemployment increased which led to high levels of repossessions and property prices dropped in value. It took the market about six years to recover to the pre-crisis levels. In the REITs stock market, the rewards are high but the risk of stock shares dropping is high as well, as discussed previously, in chapter 8. The key risks for real estate investment are as follows:

- Price tends to change
- Property tax may change
- Voids can affect your ROI
- Interest rate changes
- Properties require maintenance and repairs regularly. Unpredictable repairs may result in high losses
- Monthly mortgage payments may increase in the case of a tracker mortgage as mentioned previously, which implies more financial commitment

Figure 14.3 Average property prices during 1970 to 2020 for all types – Adapted from the Land Registry[26]

A high-risk property investor is not restricted to safe investment. Such an investor should plan to mitigate certain losses such as rental voids in order to maximise their profits and improve their portfolio. Managing tenants and collecting rents is not an easy, straightforward task. High-risk investors might face the problem of avoiding the unavoidable such as rental voids. Therefore, to mitigate the risk of voids, investors might need to

- Get actively involved in the selection process of tenants by arranging interviews before signing contracts
- Check the tenant's affordability
- Request a guarantor
- Carry out a credit check
- Avoid overcharging
- Communicate regularly with their tenants to show support and care to their families
- Invest in their property by keeping it up to scratch with regular checks and maintenance
- Keep their tenants informed about any upcoming changes and/or maintenance works
- Develop a void period strategy to minimise losses. An investor can avoid losses due to an empty income-producing property by arranging void insurance or a guaranteed rent agreement.
- Look after their employees, business operations, and management

Summary

Real estate investment and operations require careful management in terms of finances and risks. This chapter introduced the issue of risk management of real estate business and its importance for investors to analyse risk, reduce failures, and maximise the likelihood of positive results. Different asset classes can be affected by different levels of risk, and therefore require accurate risk analysis and risk tolerance measures. Investors need to acquire the necessary skills of mitigating risk to reduce any potential losses, deal with worst-case scenarios, and make sure the likelihood of getting positive outcomes is as high as possible. In this chapter, the issues of identifying and assessing risks associated with the real estate investment such as profit and loss, unexpected changes to the government's rules/regulations, or sudden changes in the market conditions have been highlighted. Due to the fact that there is no riskless investment, various topics related to risk awareness and risk tolerance have to be considered by investors during their investment journey.

Endnotes

1   Mrbanks.co.uk, https://www.mrbanks.co.uk/
    price-elasticity-of-supply
2   Economicsonline.co.uk, https://www.economicsonline.co.uk/
    Competitive_markets/The_housing_market.html
3   Danny Myers (2019), *Economics and Property*, Fourth Edition,
    Routledge, pp79–99
4   https://www.investor.gov/financial-tools-calculators/calculators/
    compound-interest-calculator
5   Albert Hirschman, https://developingeconomics.org/2019/06/24/
    hirschmans-linkages-passe-in-the-age-of-global-production-
    sharing/
6   From the Bank of England website's database page, https://
    www.bankofengland.co.uk/boeapps/database/Help.asp?Trav-
    el=NIxSUx&Back=index.asp?Travel=NIxSUx%7CFrom=Tem-
    plate%7CEC=LPMB3HD%7CG0Xtop.x=1%7CG0Xtop.y=1
7   https://hbr.org/1979/03/how-competitive-forces-shape-strategy
8   https://hbr.org/1979/03/how-competitive-forces-shape-strategy
9   https://www.churchofengland.org/resources/parish-reor-
    ganisation-and-closed-church-buildings/closed-churches/
    closed-church-buildings
10 UK Parliament, https://www.parliament.uk/business/publica-
    tions/research/key-issues-parliament-2015/social-protection/
    housing-supply/
11 The Office for National Statistics, https://www.ons.gov.uk/
    economy/inflationandpriceindices/bulletins/housepriceindex/
    september2019
12 https://www.ons.gov.uk/economy/inflationandpriceindices/
    bulletins/housepriceindex/september2019
13 https://www.ons.gov.uk/economy/inflationandpriceindices/
    bulletins/housepriceindex/september2019
14 https://landregistry.data.gov.uk/app/ukhpi/browse?-
    from=2019-12-01&location=http%3A%2F%2Flan-
    dregistry.data.gov.uk%2Fid%2Fregion%2Funited-king-
    dom&to=2020-12-01&lang=en#property_type
15 UK HPI, https://landregistry.data.gov.uk/app/ukhpi/
    browse?from=2019-12-01&location=http%3A%2F%2Flan-
    dregistry.data.gov.uk%2Fid%2Fregion%2Funited-king-
    dom&to=2020-12-01&lang=en#property_type
16 For more on the Pareto Principle see https://www.investopedia.
    com/terms/1/80-20-rule.asp
17 The Ansoff Matrix: https://corporatefinanceinstitute.com/
    resources/knowledge/strategy/ansoff-matrix/
18 UNEP https://www.unep.org/explore-topics/resource-efficiency/
    what-we-do/cities/sustainable-buildings

19   World Green Council, https://www.worldgbc.org/
        benefits-green-buildings

20   Research on Buying and Selling Homes, Research
        paper number BIS/283, October 2017, available
        at https://www.gov.uk/government/publications/
        buying-and-selling-homes-consumer-experience-study

21   Research on Buying and Selling Homes, Research
        paper number BIS/283, October 2017, available
        at https://www.gov.uk/government/publications/
        buying-and-selling-homes-consumer-experience-study

22   CNBC, https://www.cnbc.com/2019/05/10/wealthx-billion-
        aire-census-majority-of-worlds-billionaires-self-made.html

23   From the Bank of England website's database page, https://
        www.bankofengland.co.uk/boeapps/database/Help.asp?Trav-
        el=NIxSUx&Back=index.asp?Travel=NIxSUx%7CFrom=Tem-
        plate%7CEC=LPMB3HD%7CG0Xtop.x=1%7CG0Xtop.y=1

24   From the Bank of England website's database page, https://
        www.bankofengland.co.uk/boeapps/database/Help.asp?Trav-
        el=NIxSUx&Back=index.asp?Travel=NIxSUx%7CFrom=Tem-
        plate%7CEC=LPMB3HD%7CG0Xtop.x=1%7CG0Xtop.y=1

25   https://www.gov.uk/stamp-duty-land-tax

26   Land Registry, https://landregistry.data.gov.
        uk/app/ukhpi/browse?from=1970-01-01&loca-
        tion=http%3A%2F%2Flandregistry.data.gov.
        uk%2Fid%2Fregion%2Funited-kingdom&to=2020-12-01&lang=en

27   CNBC, https://www.cnbc.com/2019/05/10/wealthx-billion-
        aire-census-majority-of-worlds-billionaires-self-made.html

Bibliography

Here are some lists of suggested further reading, organised according to theme/subject. The lists present useful source material such as books, academic texts and publications, articles, reports and websites used in this book.

Real Estate Economics

https://www.economicsonline.co.uk/Competitive_markets/The_housing_market.html

https://www.mrbanks.co.uk

Niall Kishtainy, George Abbot, John Farndon, Frank Kennedy, James Meadway, Christopher Wallace, Marcus Weeks, *The Economics Book* (2015), DK Penguin Random House

Danny Myers (2019), *Economics and Property*, Fourth Edition, Routledge

W. Brueggeman and J. Fisher (2019), *Real Estate Finance and Investment*, 16th Edition, McGraw Hill

C. Hilber (2020), Real estate cycles – Lecture notes. Department of Geography and Environment, The London School of Economics and Political Science

https://www.bankofengland.co.uk

Assessing the Market

Office for National Statistics, www.ons.gov.uk

Dwelling Stock Estimates: 2017, England, https://www.gov.uk/government/statistics/dwelling-stock-estimates-in-england-2017

Homes England, Housing Statistics: 1 April 2018 – 30 September 2018, https://www.gov.uk/government/statistics/housing-statistics-1-april-2018-to-30-september-2018

English Housing Survey: Home ownership, 2016–17, https://assets.publishing.service.gov.uk/government/uploads/system/uploads/attachment_data/file/724323/Home_ownership.pdf

UK House Price Index: February 2019, https://www.gov.uk/government/news/uk-house-price-index-for-february-2019

http://www.domesdaybook.co.uk

Real Estate Investment

Robert T. Kiyosaki (2011), *Rich Dad Poor Dad*, PLATA Publishing

W. Brueggeman and J. Fisher (2019), *Real Estate Finance and Investments*, 16th Edition, McGraw Hill Education

Gary Keller with Dave Jenks and Jay Papasan (2005), *The Millionaire Real Estate Investor*, McGraw Hill Education

Eric Duneau (2019), *Out of The Rat Race: The Quest for Financial Freedom*

Rob Moore and Mark Homer (2016), *The 44 Most Closely Guarded Property Secrets*, Fourth Edition

Rob Dix (2020), *The Complete Guide to Property Investment: How To Survive & Thrive in The New World of Buy-To-Let*, Team Incredible Publishing

David R. Chesterfield (2017), *Property Investment: The Ultimate Guide to Property Investment for Beginners in the United Kingdom*

Aran Curry (2017), *The Property Coach: How to Grow and Mange a Profitable Portfolio and Win Financial Freedom*, Fourth Edition, The Insight Group

Grant Cardone (2011), *The 10X Rule: The Only Difference Between Success and Failure*, John Wiley & Son, Inc.

Paul McFadden (2018), *Your Property Jumpstart*, CS Publishing

How Business Works: A Graphic Guide to Business Success (2015), DK Penguin Random House www.dk.com

Garrett Sutton, Esq. (2018), *Start Your Own Corporation: Why The Rich Own Their Own Companies and Everyone Else Works for Them*, Third RDA Press Edition, RDA PRESS

The Business Book: Big Ideas Made Simple (2014), DK www.dk.com

How Money Works: The Facts Visually Explained (2017), DK, www.dk.com

Alexander Osterwalder and Yves Pigneur (2010), *Business Model Generation*, John Wiley & Son, Inc.

Roy Hedges (2012), *Running Your Own Business Made Easy*, Lawpack

Hugh Williams (2011), *101 Ways To Grow Your Business*, Second Edition, Lawpack Publishing Limited

https://www.investopedia.com/

Jan Ambrose (2020), The elephant in the room: Appalling housing conditions persist in many areas, but there is a way to ease the problem, *RICS Property Journal*, March/April 2020

Neil Cumins, How To Work Out a Property's Profitability, *Property Hub Magazine*, Pages 44–46, Issue 20, January 2020

Kizzi Nkwocha (Editor) (2017), *Financial Freedom Explained*, Third Edition, Athena Publishing and Mithra Publishing

Investment Analytics Report (2016), Nova Financial Group, https://nova.financial/property-report/london-investment-analytical-report

Real Estate Finance

W. Brueggeman and J. Fisher (2019), *Real Estate Finance and Investments*, 16th Edition, McGraw Hill Education

Ted Wainman (2015), *How To Talk Finance: Getting to Grips with the Numbers in Business*, Pearson

David Hillier, Iain Clacher, Stephen Ross, Randolph Westerfield, Bradford Jordan (2017), *Fundamentals of Corporate Finance*, Third Edition, McGraw Hill Education

Peter Atrill and Eddi McLaney (2019), *Accounting and Finance for Non-Specialists*, Eleventh Edition, Pearson

Stuart Warner and S.I. Hussain (2017), *The Finance Book*, FT Publishing

Rob Moore (2017), *Money: Know More, Make More, Give More*, John Murray Learning

Credit Explained (2019), Information Commissioner's Office (ICO), https://ico.org.uk/media/your-data-matters/documents/1282/credit-explained-dp-guidance.pdf

Property Accounting

Mark Smith (2018), *Small Business: A Complete Guide to Accounting Principles, Bookkeeping Principles and Tax for Small Businesses*

Peter Atrill and Eddie McLaney (2019), *Financial Accounting For Decision Makers*, Ninth Edition, Pearson

https://www.gov.uk/government/organisations/hm-revenue-customs/about [accessed on 16th April 2020]

https://www.gov.uk/income-tax [accessed on 16th April 2020]

https://www.gov.uk/stamp-duty-land-tax [accessed on 16th April 2020]

https://www.gov.uk/income-tax-rate [accessed on 16th April 2020]

https://www.gov.uk/guidance/stamp-duty-land-tax-buying-an-additional-residential-property [accessed on 17th April 2020]

https://www.gov.uk/guidance/capital-gains-tax-rates-and-allowances [accessed on 17th April 2020]

https://www.gov.uk/corporation-tax [accessed on 17th April 2020]

Robert Browning (2012), *Setting up and Running a Limited Company*, How To Books Ltd

Carl Bayley (2019), *Using A Property Company To Save Tax*, Taxcafe UK Ltd

Estate Agents

Damien Sinclair Jefferies (2015), *Trust Me I'm An Estate Agent*

Dirk Zeller (2017), *Success as a Real Estate Agent for Dummies*, Third Edition, For Dummies

Gary Keller with Dave Jenks and Jay Papasan (2004), *The Millionaire Real Estate Agent*, McGraw Hill Education

Risk Management

Business Risk: A Practical Guide For Board Members (2012), Institute of Directors, UK

Richard Winfield (2015), *The New Directors Handbook*, Brefi Press

https://www.investopedia.com/terms/r/riskmanagement.asp

https://corporatefinanceinstitute.com/resources/knowledge/strategy/risk-management

https://www.investopedia.com/terms/r/risktolerance.asp

https://searchdisasterrecovery.techtarget.com/definition/risk-mitigation

About the Author

Nasser Abouzakhar is a director of UK-based real estate investment company Anzar Property Group founded in May 2017. Between 2004 and 2019, Nasser worked at different universities in the UK as an academic, teaching and researching different computing-related subjects. He is a TEDx speaker, award-winning author, and has been a guest speaker on BBC Arabic for more than 100 live TV interviews. In 2019, he left his full-time job at university and focused primarily on his family real estate investment business in Manchester. His technology-focused background helped him to use different tools and systems to effectively run his company. With the support of all family members, he has successfully managed to build a good-sized property portfolio in the UK and succeeded in getting out of the rat race.

In this book, he covers the main topics related to real estate investment as well as the issues that he faced during his property investment journey. Nasser highlights the importance of creative finance for real estate investment business, which has been discussed in this book to help investors to structure investment deals in order to accumulate substantial possessions and property assets. He also provides useful information to investors on how to understand the risk associated with real estate investment, improve their knowledge of risk management and tolerance to reduce any potential losses and maximise the likelihood of positive outcomes. In his book, Nasser has used his academic skills and practical knowledge to explain the main topics necessary for university students to learn the required skills and knowledge about real estate investment and finance, supported with real-life scenarios.

www.ingramcontent.com/pod-product-compliance
Lightning Source LLC
Chambersburg PA
CBHW051910210326

41597CB00033B/6091